MW01028605

OCD AND AUTISM

by the same author

Can I tell you about OCD?
A guide for friends, family and professionals
Amita Jassi
Illustrated by Sarah Hull
ISBN 978 1 84905 381 5
eISBN 978 0 85700 736 0

of related interest

Kids in the Syndrome Mix of ADHD, LD, Autism
Spectrum, Tourette's, Anxiety, and More!
The one-stop guide for parents, teachers, and other professionals
Martin L. Kutscher, MD
With contributions from Tony Attwood, PhD and Robert R. Wolff, MD
ISBN 978 1 84905 967 1
eISBN 978 0 85700 882 4

A Guide to Mental Health Issues in Girls and
Young Women on the Autism Spectrum
Diagnosis, Intervention and Family Support
Dr Judy Eaton
ISBN 978 1 78592 092 9
eISBN 978 1 78450 355 0

OCD AND AUTISM

A CLINICIAN'S GUIDE TO ADAPTING
CBT

Ailsa Russell, Amita Jassi
and Kate Johnston

Illustrations by David Russell

Jessica Kingsley *Publishers*
London and Philadelphia

First published in 2019
by Jessica Kingsley Publishers
73 Collier Street
London N1 9BE, UK
and
400 Market Street, Suite 400
Philadelphia, PA 19106, USA

www.jkp.com

Copyright © Ailsa Russell, Amita Jassi and Kate Johnston 2019
Illustrations copyright © David Russell 2019

All rights reserved. No part of this publication may be reproduced in any material
form (including photocopying, storing in any medium by electronic means or
transmitting) without the written permission of the copyright owner except in
accordance with the provisions of the law or under terms of a licence issued in
the UK by the Copyright Licensing Agency Ltd. www.cla.co.uk or in overseas
territories by the relevant reproduction rights organisation, for details see
www.ifrro.org. Applications for the copyright owner's written permission to
reproduce any part of this publication should be addressed to the publisher.

The handouts and worksheets can be downloaded at ww.jkp.com/voucher
for personal use with this program, but may not be reproduced for any other
purposes without the permission of the publisher.

Warning: The doing of an unauthorised act in relation to a copyright work
may result in both a civil claim for damages and criminal prosecution.

Library of Congress Cataloging in Publication Data
A CIP catalog record for this book is available from the Library of Congress

British Library Cataloguing in Publication Data
A CIP catalogue record for this book is available from the British Library

ISBN 978 1 78592 379 1
eISBN 978 1 78450 728 2

Printed and bound in the United States

The handouts and worksheets are available to download
at www.jkp.com/voucher using the code KYEWAZO

CONTENTS

Acknowledgements.   7

About this Book   9

1. Introduction to Autism and Adaptations to Cognitive
    Behaviour Therapy   13

2. Assessment of OCD in Autism   31

3. **CBT Phase 1** Building Blocks for Treatment   49

4. **CBT Phase 2** Understanding and Rating Anxiety   69

5. **CBT Phase 2** Exposure and Response Prevention   93

6. **CBT Phase 3** Relapse Prevention.   117

7. Resources and References   131

    Index   136

ACKNOWLEDGEMENTS

We would like to thank all the autistic people both with and without OCD who helped us to learn and shape our practice. There are some things you cannot learn from books and we are grateful to you for the patient tuition.

We would also like to thank our colleagues, David Mataix-Cols, Miguel Angel Fullana and Hilary Mack. They are very much also the authors of this book but were too busy with the other great things they do to get involved with the writing process.

ABOUT THIS BOOK

Who is this book for?

This clinical workbook is written with the cognitive behavioural therapist in mind. We assume that you have knowledge and experience of helping people overcome obsessive compulsive disorder (OCD) using behaviour therapy and cognitive techniques. We do not assume that you have prior experience of working with people with autism. The aim of this workbook is to guide you in adapting your knowledge and skills so you can help someone with both OCD and autism. The workbook may also help you in your work with people who do not have an established clinical diagnosis of autism but who identify with aspects of the clinical presentation. This book will not serve you alone and you will need to learn about a person's autism so that you can individualise some of our suggestions. Patience and creativity will also be important. We link practice to theory at points we think it will be helpful, but this is very much intended to be a practical clinical workbook. We have included supporting references and suggestions for wider reading.

Why this book?

This book is based on a manual developed for a randomised controlled trial (RCT) investigating the usefulness of adapted cognitive behaviour therapy (CBT) for autism spectrum disorders (ASD) (Russell *et al.* 2013). Young people and adults over the age of 14 with a diagnosis of autism spectrum disorder and intellectual function in the average range who had a co-occurring diagnosis of obsessive compulsive disorder (OCD) took part in the RCT. The RCT manual was not developed for younger children or those with a significant intellectual disability who may require additional adaptations. Participants in the RCT were randomised to either adapted CBT for OCD, or anxiety management (AM). AM comprised up to 20 individual sessions with an autism experienced clinician, and participants learned about anxiety, progressive muscle relaxation and healthy habits. There was a significant effect of treatment in both groups, which means that both treatments were beneficial. One treatment was not superior to the other but there was a trend towards more of the people who had adapted CBT doing better. As well as telling us something about the RCT, it is important to note that anxiety education and anxiety management may be helpful for some people with autism and co-occurring OCD, particularly if the OCD symptoms are in the mildly severe range.

How does this book work?

This book aims to supplement evidence-based protocols and texts (e.g., Kyrios 2003; Wilhelm and Steketee 2006; March and Mulle 1998) outlining cognitive behavioural interventions for OCD. This book describes autism-specific adaptations to the standard CBT approach to OCD as outlined in these and other texts.

To get the most out of this book, we suggest that you read the first few chapters: 'Introduction to Autism and Adaptations to Cognitive Behaviour Therapy', 'Assessment of OCD in Autism' and 'CBT Phase 1: Building Blocks for Treatment' as a starting point for your intervention. The other chapters highlight a range of adaptations to standard CBT that may be useful in adapting your usual clinical practice. You may not need to make use of all the modifications with a single client. You do not need to follow the suggested order of adaptations and clinical tasks in this book.

A key theme in the adaptations is the use of visual material. We have been able to use a limited number of images in this book, and are restricted to monochrome. In clinical practice, we would suggest using colour images to make materials as engaging as possible.

Talking about pictures, we have relied on family to create some unique images for us. We are not great artists and if the person we are working with is not keen to draw, we all resort to online images, photographs and other media.

We are using two case vignettes, Harold and Tanisha, to illustrate the adaptations to practice throughout. Although both fictional, they are based on our experiences of working with this client group and we will introduce them here.

Harold

Harold is a 22-year-old man who received a diagnosis of autism when he was aged 15. Harold lives at home with his parents. He has several younger siblings. Harold left school after GCSE level. He was bullied by his peers and did not want to go to sixth-form college. He spent several years at home, not engaged in education or employment. He spent his time playing computer games and fixing up his motorbike. Harold has always been interested in motorbikes and has many magazines, pictures and mechanical projects related to this. Harold has always struggled with anxiety, tending to avoid situations which make him feel uncomfortable. On transition to secondary school, he had counting and checking rituals for several months. Support from the local child psychology service was helpful with this. More recently, Harold has expressed fears about contamination, particularly coming into contact with germs which might spread illness. This has affected family life considerably, with Harold refusing to use communal dishes and cutlery, eat food prepared by others or sit close to family members. Harold has been offered a place on a motor mechanics course at a local college. He would like to attend and qualify as a mechanic. He would like help in overcoming OCD as he does not think he can attend college because of this.

Tanisha

Tanisha is a 15-year-old girl who received her diagnosis of autism when she was 7 years old. She lives with her mother and grandparents. She is an only child. Tanisha stopped attending school one year ago due to the severity of her OCD. Her symptoms started when she transitioned to secondary school but worsened following an incident where she was told off by the school bully in front of the class. Her OCD fear is that she may turn into her school bully (transformation obsessions) and she has a fear of transporting into an alternative parallel universe. Initially, Tanisha avoided items related to school that may have come into contact with her school bully, would remove her uniform at the front door and would not bring any items from school to home. Eventually she stopped attending school completely due to her OCD. While at home she continued to engage in compulsions, including repeating rituals where she would continue to walk back and forwards over thresholds due to fears of transporting to an alternative dimension. She would engage in a range of checking rituals to make sure she had not changed into her school bully but also to check that she was not in an alternative universe, for example tapping objects, and asking family for reassurance that she was still in this universe. Tanisha has special interests in animals, particularly horses, and wants to be a vet when she grows up. She was academically doing well in school prior to the onset of her OCD and was hoping to study A-levels in order to become a vet in the future.

> The handouts and worksheets are available to download at www.jkp.com/voucher using the code KYEWAZO

Chapter 1

INTRODUCTION TO AUTISM AND ADAPTATIONS TO COGNITIVE BEHAVIOUR THERAPY

Agenda

- Introduction to autism

- What to call autism spectrum disorder?

- Adapting talking therapies for people with autism

- CBT-specific adaptations

Introduction to autism

Autism spectrum disorder (ASD) is the diagnostic label given to a neurodevelopmental condition characterised by qualitative impairments in social communication and a pattern of restricted or repetitive behaviours, interests and activities. ASD can affect people across the full range of general intellectual function. In approximately 50 per cent of people, a diagnosis of ASD is associated with intellectual disability.

The ability to notice and use the subtle aspects of communication, both spoken and unspoken, is usually affected in ASD. This reduces the ease with which people can interact socially. This can be particularly pronounced in group situations or unstructured social events.

A focus on particular activities or interests, and/or a preference for routine, certainty and sameness can mean that people with ASD struggle with the multiple, and at times unclear, demands of social, educational, workplace and other interactions. They may also have a particular focus of interest and activity which can be unusual in its intensity.

Autism spectrum disorder is highly heterogeneous, affecting individuals across different domains to varying degrees. Thus, individuals can differ according to the ease with which they communicate verbally, how much they prefer routine and certainty, how much they enjoy social situations, their focus on a particular area of interest and their understanding of emotions.

There is a large body of psychological research and a number of theoretical accounts explaining the core clinical characteristics of ASD. Notably, the research highlighting a reduced ability to understand and make inferences about the mental states of others (Theory of Mind), difficulty seeing the 'whole picture' (central coherence), emotion recognition difficulties and relative impairments in executive function ('higher level' thinking skills such as planning or flexibility) are perhaps the most relevant to verbally mediated psychological interventions. There can also be a dissociation between intellectual ability and practical living skills.

Any therapeutic situation is essentially an interpersonal, social situation, often with unclear expectations. Therapy involves meeting a new person in an unfamiliar setting. Attending therapy is anxiety provoking for most people but may be particularly so for this group. Your job as therapist is to scaffold the therapeutic situation so that you and the individual can use psychological principles and techniques to help with the presenting problem. To achieve this focus, and make best use of the opportunity for psychological intervention, it will be important to reduce the particular demands of the therapeutic context that the person may struggle with. Below we will give some ideas and suggestions for doing this.

Later in this chapter, Table 1.1 provides a quick reference guide to help you adapt your therapeutic style. We will add more detail as we move through the book.

What to call autism spectrum disorder?

Until 2013, diagnostic labels included Asperger's syndrome, autism, high-functioning autism, atypical autism, and pervasive developmental disorder, among others. Epidemiological and genetic studies have highlighted that the distinctions between these different labels may be artificial, and that the symptom states and trajectories are far more fluid than previously thought. Thus, ascribing a single overarching diagnostic label of autism spectrum disorder according to the *Diagnostic and Statistical Manual of Mental Disorders, version 5* (DSM-5) (American Psychiatric Association 2013) has become the convention in many clinics. Individuals may historically have received a different label and prefer to continue to use it. Additionally, there are different views and preferences as to what constitutes an acceptable label (Kenny *et al.* 2016). Some members of the autism community have expressed dissatisfaction with use of the word 'disorder' and its implication that there is something wrong that needs to be amended. Disability rights advocates suggest that autism is better thought of as a difference to be embraced alongside other individual differences. The spectrum is also not confined to those who receive a clinical diagnosis, and there is a body of research suggesting that autism traits are distributed across the population.

The term you use to denote an individual's ASD (if needed at all) may impact on the therapeutic alliance. If you strike on use of a label or form of words that jars with an individual, they might struggle to accept your best intentions as a psychological therapist. Where possible, it is a good idea to set out on the therapeutic endeavours with your individual client by enquiring how they prefer you to address autism spectrum disorder and to learn how it affects them as an individual. Some people are not in agreement with the diagnosis they have received and do not identify themselves as autistic.

In this workbook, we use the terms autism and autistic people. For example, you might from the outset ask your client:

How do you refer to autism? What words would you prefer we use?

What do I need to know about how autism (or preferred label) affects you as an individual?

Ask about communication preferences:

What about the way that we are communicating right now? Am I using the right words, talking at the right speed, explaining things in a way that makes sense? Is there anything that is difficult to understand? What do familiar people you understand clearly do when communicating that is different to what I am doing?

Sometimes it can be helpful to contract particular aspects of communication. You can explain that at times you might need to interrupt to keep the session on-track. You can say something like:

As we only have a limited time when we meet, I will be trying to make sure we get through all of the material we need to. In order to do this, I might sometimes need to interrupt you so that we can finish the important parts of each session. This is not because I'm not interested in what you have to say, but it is so that we stay focused on the things that might help improve your OCD.

Or:

It is important that I hear about the things you enjoy doing and what you are interested in or the struggles that you have each week that are not related to your OCD. We do need to make sure we have enough time each week to work on the OCD. I wonder if we could spend the first (or last) ten minutes reviewing your week in general before we move on to talk about the OCD.

Interests and routines:

Was there something you needed to do before you came here today?

Do you have any routines that take up lots of your day?

Apart from the OCD, would you be upset if there were particular things you couldn't do every day? Is there anything that you have to do in a specific or particular way?

Do you have things that you are very interested in that you spend lots of time thinking or learning about or doing?

Issues with daily living or other problems:

It is helpful for me to know a bit about the things you need to do to look after yourself, like washing, dressing, buying food, cooking, paying bills, looking after where you live, housework. Lots of people find some of these things difficult. Do you struggle with any of these sorts of things? Do you receive help from anyone with daily living tasks?

Are there any other important issues you want me to be aware of that would be useful to our work together?

You can use the worksheet 'What do I need to know about your autism?' if that seems suitable.

WORKSHEET: WHAT DO I NEED TO KNOW ABOUT YOUR AUTISM?

Communication	**Do you have any communication preferences or needs?**

What do I need to know about communicating with you?

☐ _____

☐ _____

☐ _____

Examples:

☐ I tend to take things literally so you should not be too vague

☐ I don't like people to use certain words

☐ I find it hard to understand jokes so please do not make any

Interests and routines	**Do you have any particular routines that are important to you?**

What is it helpful to know?

☐ _____

☐ _____

☐ _____

Examples:

☐ I have an all-encompassing interest in Dr Who, that is an important part of my life

☐ I might talk about my interest and might not want to miss certain events so it is helpful if people working with me understand this

☐ I have a morning routine that I need to do every day and so I cannot have appointments before 10am

Daily living	**Do you find any specific daily activities difficult?**

What is it helpful to know?

☐ _____

☐ _____

☐ _____

Examples:

☐ I dislike being in crowded places

☐ I find socialising stressful

☐ I don't like fluorescent lighting

Adapting talking therapies for people with autism

There are some adaptations that are inspired by the core characteristics of autism and which are relevant to all talking therapies, regardless of theoretical orientation.

Some adaptations are CBT-specific and include changes to the content and structure as well as the delivery of CBT.

Shared communication

It is essential to develop a shared understanding of the problem and potential solution. You may have to spend time getting to know how the individual communicates more generally, before moving on to find out how they communicate and think about the problem that is OCD and the relevant emotions. Once a good communicative rapport has been established, it is then possible to embark on the process of getting to know the OCD.

You may have to adjust your *verbal communication style*. Open questions may not elicit an elaborate response and the flow of conversation may not be fluent. You may find that the use of open questions to guide the conversation, i.e. guided discovery or Socratic dialogue, is unhelpful.

You might find that you have to ask a lot of questions to get the information needed for an assessment and formulation. Try to be patient, ask a question and wait for an answer before asking a follow-up question. If an answer is not immediately forthcoming, the individual might be processing your question and formulating their response; something that can be slower in people with autism. If you throw another question in the mix, this increases the verbal demands of the situation further.

If questions yield minimal or yes/no responses, try and use closed or forced choice questions to gather the information needed; for example, *'Is the urge to wash your hands greater when you are at work or when you are at home?'* Using a visual prompt can be helpful at times so that an individual can point to an answer rather than needing to verbalise if this is their preference.

There may be less talk about emotional states and more talk about external events and explanations for problems in the early stages of therapy.

There may be a discrepancy between expressive and receptive language. Check you are understanding each other using summaries and asking your client to paraphrase.

There may be idiosyncratic use of language, particularly when describing emotional states. The term anxiety might be an unfamiliar label. For example, an individual might describe anxiety as *'the inside is bigger than the outside'* or may use a different emotion word altogether (such as anger). You and the individual client will have to develop a shared communication strategy about emotional states, preferably using the client's language. Again, this can be supported with visual cues or prompts if this is the client's preference.

Try to avoid using abstract language or metaphors. The tendency to make literal interpretations of language can lead to misunderstandings. For example:

T: *Hello John, you look like you're a bit under the weather today.*

John: *Well, I'm always under the weather unless I'm at the top of a mountain, aren't I? I don't understand why people say that.*

Alternatively, you may have to adjust your *non-verbal communication style*.

Making eye contact might be aversive. A directly facing posture, leaning forward and using your body language to convey empathy and facilitate engagement may be off-putting. Subtle changes in facial expression may be misunderstood or missed completely. Be aware that eye contact may be too much or minimal, which can leave the client feeling uncomfortable.

Sit calmly at a 90-degree angle, continue verbal communication in the absence of eye contact and maintain a clear, positive facial expression. Clear smiles convey positive regard and an indication that the therapeutic session is progressing well.

Engagement

As with any other client group, the therapeutic relationship developed between therapist and individual client is fundamental to a successful intervention. You may find it harder to gauge the degree of alliance formed, however, due to the differences in reciprocal social interaction which are part of autism. Don't be discouraged or have expectations of social reciprocity, particularly in early sessions. Checking in with clients at the end of each session may help to establish things that you could do differently to facilitate engagement.

Autistic clients may find the initial therapeutic meeting or assessment sessions more confusing or anxiety provoking than other people. The therapy situation is generally a new, inter-personal situation and thus the type of situation where the core characteristics of autism are likely to be more in evidence. As a therapist, you can ease the situation by being patient and gentle in your approach and clear about the expectations of this new situation.

The initial session(s) may involve no more than getting to know the individual, their style of communication, their personal history, support network and daily routines. We would encourage an extended period of engagement, and this might require two or three sessions.

You may find that your client does not become self-generated in applying treatment principles. You might need to be more directive in your therapeutic style, outlining concrete, specific and rule-bound therapeutic tasks to aid generalisation. That is ok, it does not mean you or your client have not done a good job, it is simply in line with their needs.

Structure, timings and treatment duration

The inherent structure of CBT is often very helpful for people with autism. There is an established and clear routine for sessions (i.e., agenda setting) and for the overall intervention (i.e., assessment, formulation, goal-setting). These aspects of CBT are important to establish at the outset and will be helpful to you and your client.

Try and make appointments at the same time and on the same day of the week if you can. This consistency will be helpful to the client in remembering appointments and building the sessions into a weekly routine. Remember that executive function difficulties, including organisation and planning, can accompany autism, and minimising demands on these can be helpful.

You may find that sessions are slightly longer or slightly shorter than usual. Some people may not tolerate lengthy sessions, others may need more time to absorb information and consider concepts. Some individuals will prefer shorter sessions, experiencing the dual demands of processing interpersonal information and 'doing CBT' to be exhausting (Anderson and Morris 2006).

There is also some research that suggests a reduction of anxiety may take a bit longer in autistic people and hence any exposure-based sessions should leave sufficient time to allow resolution of the anxious response.

Due to a longer and broader assessment, and the possible inclusion of additional sessions for psycho-education, you may find that your client needs a longer treatment period than you usually offer. We outline a treatment plan which can be delivered across a potential maximum of 20 sessions. Not all participants in the RCT needed all 20 sessions, but some did require a longer treatment duration to make and consolidate progress.

Therapist: keep it organised, keep it visual

- Provide written or typed session summaries.

- Provide a folder where the person can keep the material.

- Make the summaries and handouts as visual as possible.

- Use the person's preferred visual images and analogies.

Treatment setting

As far as possible, use the same clinic room when you can. New physical environments can produce sensory overload for autistic people, and processing a new room with differences in colours, furniture, lighting and noise each week will take up valuable time in sessions. A familiar room (so long as it is suitable) will be helpful to the routine of therapy.

You may need to model exposure tasks, or non-OCD performance of behaviours. You will also want to carry out in vivo work as much as possible during the change elements of this intervention (taking the work out of the office, and into real life as much as possible). This may involve leaving the clinic room.

Table 1.1: Some tips for therapeutic style

	Try to...				Try not to...		
Communication	Use visual aids or tools. Don't be afraid to draw or use colour.	Use concrete language. Use forced choice if open questions do not elicit good information.	Allow time for the individual to process your communication, and to form a response. Check that you understand each other.	Summarise the key points you have been talking about a few times per session. Check out idiosyncratic uses of language, e.g. what emotion does 'pressure in the head' refer to?	Use non-verbal communication, e.g. 'lean in' and make eye contact.	Use abstract concepts, metaphors or figures of speech, e.g. moving the goalposts.	Assume expressive and receptive language are at the same level in any individual.
Social interaction	Don't worry if engagement seems a bit 'different'.	Be clear about the expectations of the 'social' (therapy) situation.	Explain that you might need to interrupt or ask certain things.		Expect fluid and easy social interaction.	Use too much 'small talk'.	

cont.

	Try to...				Try not to...	
Executive function	Be clear about the 'where, when and who' when planning novel tasks such as homework.	Plan activities together in a way that the individual thinks will work for them. Review and update these in session.	Follow the structure of session.		Assume that the individual will generalise from one setting to another.	
Repetitive behaviours	Develop a routine in the session.	Anticipate anxiety – particularly if new situations are planned.	Take a graded approach to introducing changes in behaviour.	Use special interests as a tool to convey concepts.	Plan activities or sessions which interfere with interests and routines.	Let special interests or accounts of routines dominate.
Alexithymia	Check out the individual's level of literacy with the problem emotion(s).	Use visual aids and colour for 'shades' of emotion.	Develop an individualised feelings rating scale (with descriptors).	Practise using the rating scale in sessions.	Talk about feelings and emotions in general terms.	Assume the individual is aware of subtle changes in emotional states.

CBT-specific adaptations

We have used the basic 'thoughts-feelings-behaviour' framework to depict how we understand the things you might need to do differently, such as the adaptations to the content and structure of CBT to render it more accessible for autistic people. As we move through the workbook, the examples will provide a bit more detail.

The rationale, however, is as follows. Thoughts in CBT are essentially verbal representations of abstract, internal phenomena. They are not tangible but can be important drivers of feeling states and behaviour. Cognitive techniques in CBT encourage the therapist and client to explore thoughts and related cognitive processes. This is an abstract verbal activity at the outset, albeit one which can develop into behaviourally oriented experiments as treatment progresses. Literal, concrete use and understanding of language is a feature of autism.

Executive function is the umbrella term for a set of neuro-psychological processes involved in future-oriented behaviour. Research has found impairments in a number of executive functions in autism, particularly in cognitive flexibility, generativity and planning. Generating and shifting to alternative ways of thinking may be inherently difficult for autistic people. As a consequence, there is an emphasis on changing behaviour rather than cognitions in autism-adapted CBT (NICE 2012). In the context of OCD, this means relying on exposure and response prevention (ERP) as the main change technique. ERP describes the process whereby an individual enters anxiety-provoking situations in a planned and often graded manner (exposure) and refrains from engaging in the rituals or compulsions that they usually use in those situations (response prevention).

Feelings in CBT means noticing changes in emotional states. This relies on interoceptive awareness and introspective processes, i.e. noticing changes in bodily sensations, identifying and labelling these in respect of emotional state changes, and noticing the antecedents. Studies suggest that such processes may be different in autistic people, although the present state of the evidence is inconclusive as to precisely at what level these differences may lie.

Nonetheless, the ability to notice and label changes in feelings is an important prerequisite for CBT. Emotional literacy is an important area for assessment in autism-adapted CBT. In the case of OCD, this is anxiety literacy in particular. Psycho-education is often needed to put foundation skills in place before embarking on the 'change' components of CBT.

Behaviour change is ultimately the goal of cognitive behaviour therapy and paves the road to reducing psychological distress as well as individual goal attainment. The inherent preference for routine, sameness and certainty may mean change is not easily embraced by autistic people and may be a source of anxiety or concern. Furthermore, behaviour change in CBT is often the domain of between-session homework tasks where the therapist is not available. Novel behaviours require planning and flexibility, and the executive function difficulties in autism may make this difficult. Consequently, adaptations to scaffold and support behaviour change in CBT are needed and change may occur at a more gradual and graded pace.

Executive function impairments:
Cognitive flexibility
Planning, generativity

Language:
Literal interpretation

Relevant adaptations:
Emphasis on changing behaviour
rather than cognitions
Scaffolds for behaviour change

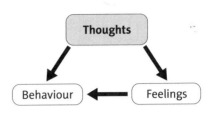

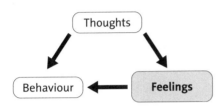

Emotional literacy:
Alexithymia/Emotion recognition
(self and others)

Relevant adaptation:
Enhance emotional literacy prior to
change elements of CBT

Repetitive behaviours:
Preference for routine
Restricted repertoire of activities
Circumscribed interests

Relevant adaptations:
Therapist awareness
Graded change
Support novel behaviours

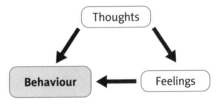

Chapter 2

ASSESSMENT OF OCD IN AUTISM

Agenda

- General guidance for assessing OCD in people with autism

- Suggested routine for assessment session(s)

- The structured clinical interview: getting to know the OCD

- What if the client can't describe how they feel?

- Standardised self-report measures

- Therapist tips

General guidance for assessing OCD in people with autism

Assessment in cognitive behaviour therapy tends to focus on the problem specifics, often moving swiftly to get a detailed account of a recent problem episode.

Assessment adapted for autism tends to take a broader, more holistic, approach (at least initially). This has several aims:

- To establish rapport and assess communication style.

- To gain a sense of the individual's daily routine, preference for sameness, special interests and support network. This will inform intervention plans as well as the assessment.

- To assess anxiety-based obsessions and compulsions, and distinguish these from repetitive thoughts, behaviours and routines characteristic of autism.

- To gain an understanding of the individual's emotional literacy and develop a shared means of talking about emotional states.

- To consider how best to measure the anxiety-based obsessions and compulsions at baseline

Key considerations

- Disentangling anxiety-based, ego-dystonic (thoughts, images, urges and behaviour repugnant and distressing to a person and not in keeping with their character) OCD symptoms from the repetitive behaviours characteristic of ASD.

- Increased prevalence of other commonly co-occurring conditions (e.g., social anxiety, depression, Gilles de la Tourette syndrome).

- Difficulty responding to open questions.

- Difficulty talking/thinking abstractly, for example about antecedents or triggers to an event that has already occurred.

- Differences in memory recall.

- Difficulty reporting on own thoughts and feelings, for example difficulty accessing content of obsessive thoughts or not reporting obsessions at all.

- Frequently, but not always, the client may not show a great deal of insight into the excessive nature of compulsive rituals, or show any awareness of what are typical and atypical thought processes and emotional states.

Suggested routine for assessment session(s)
Building rapport

- Introduce yourself to the client as well as parents or carers if they are present.

- Explain your role.

- Provide an overview of the session.

- Be sensitive to the fact that the client may be feeling very anxious.

- Remember that the client may not be familiar with the therapist–client relationship and that this unique relationship may be particularly confusing to autistic people.

- Ensure that you make the session as predictable as possible by establishing an agenda and being clear about how long it will last. Discuss the individual's preferences for how to talk about autism and what you need to know about their autism.

Please note that if the client is so anxious and 'resistant' to the idea that their obsessions and compulsions are a problem, or if their style of communication is making it difficult to get to grips with the problem, this session would be best spent simply developing a rapport and getting to know the person in a more general sense, rather than focusing on OCD.

Meeting with the client individually
Assess OCD symptoms

- Establish what are the client's current and most problematic symptoms of OCD and the severity of these using a structured clinical interview and/or standardised self-report measures. This is described in detail later in this chapter.

Explore views on OCD and anxiety

- Gain some understanding of the client's view of their OCD – for example, do they see it as a problem, what is their model for the problem?

- Explore the client's experience of, and language for, anxiety and discomfort. How do they describe this, and how does it affect them?

- Establish if they can differentiate between thoughts, feelings and behaviour.

- Ask the client what they have tried so far, what works, what doesn't work.

Review mental state and general functioning

- Gain some initial knowledge about the client's daily routine, social networks, preferred activities and so on. You may need this information to assist with treatment at a later stage (e.g., ritual replacement with preferred, diverting activities).

- Assess mood – how is the client feeling at this point in time? If they are significantly depressed, this may have implications for treatment.

- Offer an opportunity for the client to ask questions.

Meeting with the parent, partner or carer (if relevant and the client gives permission)

- Establish how the parent/carer perceives the main symptoms.

- Ask about parent/carer's involvement in compulsions (e.g., providing reassurance).

- Investigate the parent/carer's beliefs about the client's fears (e.g., does the parent/carer hold similar beliefs about the likelihood and consequences of contamination?).

- Ask how the parent/carer is coping in general.

- Ask about the individual client's coping skills and what happens when they are very anxious and uncomfortable.

- Consider any risk issues.

The structured clinical interview: getting to know the OCD

OCD is a disabling mental disorder characterised by obsessions or compulsions or both. Obsessions are repeated, unwanted, intrusive thoughts, images and urges which the individual experiences as repugnant and which cause anxiety. Compulsions are repeated acts (behavioural or mental) that the individual feels compelled to do in response to an obsession or according to rigid rules. Compulsions aim to prevent a feared event or to reduce anxiety. Avoidance of stimuli and situations that trigger obsessions and compulsions is a core feature of OCD. Obsessions and compulsions are normal everyday phenomena, which are considered pathological if they occupy more than one hour of waking time.

It is generally a good idea to use a structured symptom checklist such as the Yale-Brown Obsessive Compulsive Scale – Symptom Checklist (Y-BOCS) (Goodman *et al.* 1989). For young people aged 17 years and below, use the Children's Yale-Brown Obsessive Compulsive Scale (CY-BOCS) (Goodman *et al.* 1991).

It is important to establish from the outset that the client understands what is meant by obsessions and compulsions, and that the enquiry is not about obsessions as *'something one is very interested in'* and repetitive acts/behaviours where anxiety reduction is not the primary purpose. Begin the interview by asking what a person understands by obsessions and compulsions, for example, *'What do you think is meant by an obsession?'* If the client does not offer a definition consistent with OCD by saying, for example, *'It is something you are very interested in'*, ensure that you clarify what you mean by an obsession, for example by saying, *'Yes, that is true, but there is another meaning to obsession and that is what I am going to be asking you about. An obsession can refer to an unwanted thought, image or urge that comes into your mind even when you don't want it to, and makes you feel uncomfortable.'* Give examples of obsessions, and ask the person if there is anything they worry about or feel they need to do that sounds a bit like this.

When enquiring about symptom types as listed on the Y-BOCS (Goodman *et al.* 1989), it may be important to ask specific concrete questions, rather than making a general enquiry about the need to do certain things in a certain way. For example, one may have learned about an individual's fear of contamination and washing rituals, but the individual may not make an association between that problem and another similar area of difficulty. The therapist may need to enquire about specific daily routines in order to establish if there are other areas where the client feels compelled to do certain things. For example, *'So after you have showered and dressed, what happens next? What do you have for breakfast? Is there anything you need to do in the kitchen before, during or after breakfast? What did you need to do before you came here today?'*

Your client may find it difficult to think beyond the present moment or problem and describe to you the sorts of situations or events where the problem is triggered or gets worse. You may need to do some detective work and enquire about how the day has gone so far, ask them to talk about everything they did leading up to an event or situation and develop a narrative of the problem in this way.

You may need to ask the client with ASD and OCD more frequently than other clients how it feels if they don't do the behaviour.

It may also be helpful to ask closed questions and offer options/forced choice for possible answers, for example if there is no response to your *'How does it feel?'* question, you might prompt with, *'Would you feel comfortable or uncomfortable if you did not do the behaviour?'* and continue to work in this way until you are happy that you have a good sense of what happens for the individual.

Disentangling OCD symptoms from repetitive behaviours

Repetitive behaviour is a descriptive term referring to behaviour which is repeated in an invariant manner, is topographically consistent, and appears functionless in that its meaning is not immediately clear to the observer (Turner 1999). The term restricted repetitive behaviours (RRB) in autism encompasses a wide range of behavioural phenomena from motor stereotypies, such as rocking or self-biting, to adherence to a complex sequence of routines to repeated thoughts or preoccupation with and difficulty shifting a pattern of thinking or belief system. Clearly the presence of RRB can be a confounder when assessing OCD symptoms, given their similarities.

It is helpful to become familiar with the phenomenology encompassed by the RRB domain in autism. The Autism Diagnostic Interview-Revised (ADI-R) (Lord, Rutter and Le Couteur 1994) outlines ten categories:

1. Encompassing preoccupation or circumscribed pattern of interest.

2. Apparently compulsive adherence to non-functional routines or rituals.

3. Unusual sensory interests.

4. Undue general sensitivity to noise.

5. Abnormal, idiosyncratic negative response to specific sensory stimuli.

6. Difficulties with minor changes in routine or personal environment.

7. Resistance to trivial changes in the environment.

8. Unusual attachment to objects.

9. Stereotyped and repetitive hand and finger and other motor mannerisms.

10. Preoccupation with parts of object/non-functional elements of material.

These different categories of RRB have been conceptualised as representing two factors, 'lower-order', repetitive sensory-motor behaviours and 'higher-order', insistence on sameness behaviours. General ability and language levels are important confounds in the expression of RRB (for a review see Leekham, Prior and Uljarevic 2011).

Autistic people and co-occurring OCD will have repetitive behaviours as part of autism. It can take a clinician some time to disentangle the routines and rituals that are symptoms of OCD and thus suitable foci for intervention.

Some individuals are able to explain clearly which routines are anxiety based, and a response to intrusive worries and concerns. Other people find this more difficult, particularly in describing how they feel inside when able, or not able, to carry out an action.

Assessment of OCD in autism usually involves a structured clinical interview, standardised measures in the form of self-report questionnaires and gathering corroborating information from someone who knows the person well, such as a spouse, parent or carer. Taking a history of the behavioural phenomena in question can be hugely important.

There are no quick or sure-fire routes to tell the difference between OCD and RRB, but we have found the following points useful.

First, study the phenomenology of the behaviour. A compulsion in the OCD sense is *purposeful* in that it typically serves to prevent a dreaded event (e.g., *'If I don't check the oven is switched off* (compulsion), *a fire might start and the house will burn down'*) and to reduce the anxiety provoked by this obsessional thought or worry. Compulsions can be distressing in themselves. They can vary across time, place and setting in response to the situational context and presence of anxiety-provoking triggers. Repetitive behaviours are typically described as unvarying, topographically consistent and not particularly pertinent to the individual's

current situation or context. Little is known abℓ
repetitive behaviours (RB), but to the observer they
purposeless. It is also not clear if RRB are anxiety ℓ
pleasure inducing and this may differ across individuals. ℎℓ
RRB should not be particularly connected to a situation or feℓ
event and should present as independent of clear triggers anℓ
situations apart from those which permit or induce the behaviour.
For example, in the case of RRB, the sight of running water may
stimulate a young person to run their hands under the water in a
stereotyped manner for a long time, with a certain degree of visual
fixation. They might take every opportunity available to engage in
this behaviour. In the case of OCD, the person will only run their
hands under the water if they are concerned that they have become
contaminated – if an obsession about germs or dirt has been
triggered – and it is likely to be clear that they are 'washing' their
hands rather than enjoying the water. It has been our experience
that autistic adults report specific OCD-related beliefs, such as, *'If I
open the door with my hands and don't wash them straight away with
disinfecting soap, I will pick up germs, get ill and have to go to hospital'*
in the same way that other people with OCD do. Compulsions as
part of OCD are generally acts that individuals report they have to
complete 'correctly', according to a set of rules or criteria such as
'until it feels right'. To our knowledge, factors accounting for the
onset and offset of RRB are yet to be accounted for.

Second, the *onset* and *course* of the behavioural phenomena can
reveal important information. The onset of a 'new' phenomenon in
adolescence or adulthood is more likely to be an anxiety disorder
such as OCD than part of autism. Repetitive behaviours are part of
early development in all children but persist in children with autism.
'Lower-order' RRB, such as motor stereotypies, tend to reduce
over the course of development, while higher-level insistence on
sameness behaviours persist through adolescence into adulthood
(e.g., Chowdhury, Benson and Hillier 2010). OCD has a bi-modal
onset, around puberty or early adulthood (e.g., Geller *et al.* 1998).
Just when repetitive behaviours start to drop off in autism, the risk

of OCD is increased. Any new phenomenon in early adolescence or later that represents a break with childhood patterns of repetition is more likely to be OCD than a new repetitive behaviour.

Third, the *form* the behaviour takes may not reveal a great deal of helpful information. Studies of children and adults with ASD have not noted anything autism-specific about the OCD symptoms in this group. However, this does mean that behaviour which looks like typical OCD is more likely to be OCD than anything else.

In our experience, the most problematic OCD symptom dimensions to disentangle from repetitive behaviours are:

- symmetry, ordering, counting and arranging obsessions and compulsions versus a preference for routine and sameness

- hoarding versus collecting as part of a special interest.

Remember Tanisha, the 15-year-old girl with transformation obsessions and fear of being transported to another dimension? One of Tanisha's rituals was to move things around in her home, especially her bedroom, and tap different surfaces. Her therapist conducted an assessment to establish if these were RB as part of autism or OCD. In order to establish this, a developmental assessment was completed with her family to get a timeline of symptoms. From this they recognised that while she had engaged in ordering and arranging rituals since she was very young, the type of behaviours they were seeing now were new and started around a year ago and were accompanied by other new behaviours such as getting stuck in doorways and avoiding school-related materials.

The therapist met with Tanisha to explore this further. The therapist completed some psycho-education on different emotions and Tanisha was able to say she noticed her heart racing when she was anxious. The therapist explored the following with her:

T: *So let's think about yesterday when you were in your bedroom and you were moving your books on your shelf. Before you did that, did you get any bad thoughts in your head or feel anxious?*

Tanisha: *What do you mean?*

T: *Did you notice your heart started to beat quickly when you were in your bedroom at 6pm before you started to move things on your bookshelf?*

Tanisha: *I think so.*

T: *Did you get any horrible thoughts pop into your head beforehand?*

Tanisha: *What do you mean?*

T: *Did you think something bad would happen if you did not move things around on your bookshelf.*

Tanisha: *I think so.*

T: *Was it annoying to have to move things around in your bedroom?*

Tanisha: *No, I liked it.*

T: *Did you like it while you were moving them around or did you like it because it made the scary thought go away and your heart rate go down?*

Tanisha: *Yes, actually that's what it is, the thought went away when I got it just right.*

T: *Do you wish you did not have to move things around?*

Tanisha: *No, I would be scared, but it is annoying.*

The therapist has to use closed questions and forced choices to gather the information necessary to establish the basis of the behaviour.

What if the client can't describe how they feel?

This is not uncommon. At the assessment stage, you need only concentrate on finding out if the feeling state is pleasant or unpleasant. If it is the latter, try to elicit a concrete description of the feeling state.

How would you feel if you could not do that behaviour? or *How does it make you feel when the worry comes into your mind?*

Is the feeling comfortable or uncomfortable?

Do you notice any changes in your body?

You can use directive, closed questions such as:

Does your heart rate speed up?

This is where a body map comes in useful. Ask the client to mark where on their body they notice the feelings using a simple outline drawing of a body map (see worksheet). You can ask a bit more about each body area they mark to find out what they notice, for example heart racing faster. The physiological symptoms of anxiety will become evident in this way. Once these are clear, summarise the bodily changes and ask, *'What word do you use to describe it when your body feels this way?'*

Standardised self-report measures

In addition to routine outcome measurement, self-report measures can provide helpful information about OCD symptom dimensions, capture information about co-occurring problems and provide a very preliminary index of an individual's emotional literacy. We list some measures we find helpful below.

Recommended measures

- Obsessive-Compulsive Inventory-Revised (OCI-R) – use the normative data for autistic adults (Cadman *et al.* 2015). A cut-off score of 29 on the OCI-R gave a sensitivity score of 69 per cent and specificity of 70 per cent, so although not perfect, it is helpful to note that the average score of an autistic person without a clinical diagnosis of OCD is higher than usual on the OCI-R.

- For young people aged 18 years and under, the Children's Obsessive-Compulsive Inventory-Revised (ChOCI-R) can be used (Uher *et al.* 2008). To our knowledge there is no data specifically on the use of this tool with young people with autism.

- Take a measure of social anxiety – standardised questionnaires such as the Liebowitz Social Anxiety Scale (Liebowitz 1987) or the Social Phobia Inventory for adults (Connor *et al.* 2000) or the Spence Children's Anxiety Scale (Spence 1998) are generally helpful. This is because social anxiety and other areas of anxiety are very common in ASD and they may impact on the treatment of the OCD.

- High rates of depression are reported across the lifespan in autism. Take a measure of mood using the Patient Health Questionnaire-9 (PHQ-9) (Kroenke, Spitzer and Williams 2001) or the Beck Depression Inventory (Beck, Steer and Brown 1996). For young people, you can use the Mood and Feelings Questionnaire (Angold and Costello 1987) or the Revised Children's Anxiety and Depression Scale (Chorpita *et al.* 2000).

- There are high rates of family involvement and accommodation of OCD symptoms. A good way to measure this is the Family Accommodation Scale (Calvocoressi *et al.* 1999).

Key considerations in use of standardised measures

- The client may have difficulty accessing content of obsessive thoughts or not report obsessions at all.

- The client may rate all symptoms at 'extreme' on severity ratings due to difficulty perceiving graduations in their own emotional arousal.

- The client may feel uncomfortable with 'pen and paper' self-report measures due to processing of written material and handwriting.

- Paper and pencil measures can sometimes elicit a more accurate self-report than a verbal interview and can be a good place to start finding out about the nature of the problem if verbal communication is difficult.

- Problems choosing between items and being easily distracted can be an issue. If this seems the case, cover up all items except the current one to be addressed.

Therapist tips

- Use a symptom checklist such as that contained within the Yale-Brown Obsessive Compulsive Scale to ascertain the areas of concern. It is unusual for OCD to manifest in only one symptom area, so using a concrete list of commonly described obsessions and compulsions can be useful. There is evidence in the literature that autistic people with co-occuring OCD do not differ significantly in symptom type from other people with OCD.

- Involve parents or carers in the assessment as a source of collateral information.

- Take a history of the phenomena, including onset and course. A timeline may be helpful as it provides a visual representation of time across which to map relevant events.

- Opt for a longer, more gradual assessment if clients become overwhelmed by extended questioning.

- Vary the assessment approach to fit the client's preferred way of disclosing information (e.g., some clients may prefer written modality such as email).

- Be mindful that intrusive, unwanted thoughts may be even more upsetting and frightening for autistic clients, and they may be more reluctant to discuss obsessional thoughts, or less able to reflect objectively about thoughts than other clients.

- Remember that parent/carer modelling is likely to be important in the client's recovery from OCD so it is important to establish whether the parent/carer has any beliefs that may undermine treatment.

- Be alert at this stage to the content of special interests, which may be useful later as a tool with which to translate psychological concepts.

- Use in vivo techniques to place the client in a situation that causes mild discomfort to see if the client can then report 'hot thoughts' or physiological reactions if self-report is really a problem.

- Remember that an impoverished daily routine and limited repertoire of interests and activities may mean that compulsive rituals do not interfere with 'everyday' function in a way that enhances the development of insight.

WORKSHEET: EXAMPLE BODY MAP

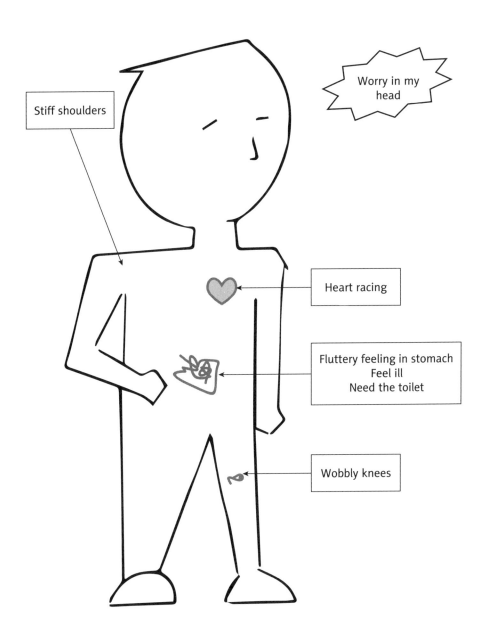

Worry in my head

Stiff shoulders

Heart racing

Fluttery feeling in stomach
Feel ill
Need the toilet

Wobbly knees

Chapter 3

CBT PHASE I BUILDING BLOCKS FOR TREATMENT

Agenda

- Treatment overview
- Goal setting
- OCD psycho-education
- Formulation
- Therapist tips

Treatment overview

Treatment will vary according to individual need. You may find that treatment progresses slowly and that the early building blocks (psycho-education) are essential before a client can progress to exposure and response prevention (ERP). You may also find that some clients do not need the early stages and can progress quickly to ERP. Ideally, this will be an outcome of the assessment but it is not always the case. Sometimes you learn about the need to make adaptations because treatment does not progress easily. However, it is advisable to check that the building blocks for CBT (i.e., emotional literacy) are in place. A high-functioning, verbal client with many skills may still struggle significantly with emotion recognition and it is a good idea to check out their skills in this area and not make assumptions. You do not want to embark on ERP without being confident that your client can notice and rate different intensities of anxiety.

The list of treatment components is ordered according to a rough sequence. Techniques that tend to be used early in therapy are listed first, but it is not intended that therapists work through them all, in order, from beginning to end.

In terms of an overall treatment structure, it is expected that treatment might progress in the following manner once the assessment is complete:

Sessions 1–3	Assessment and engagement
Session 4	Goal setting and brief introduction to treatment model
Sessions 4–6	Anxiety education, recognition, rating Model of OCD and the role of anxiety exposure – how does it work
Sessions 6–7	Building a hierarchy for OCD
Sessions 8–9	Commence ERP in session
Sessions 10–18	Move up the hierarchy using ERP
Session 19–20	Maintenance and relapse prevention

Set a clear and consistent session length so the client knows what to expect, but be aware that this may vary on an individual basis. Some people might prefer a short session. Others may require longer sessions to allow extra time for slower information-processing or pedantic, long-winded speech patterns.

Key considerations

- Provide an overview of the CBT approach to the treatment of OCD if appropriate at this stage. Try and use the client's language/model to convey the psychological concepts where possible.

- Explain that treatment starts with the development of skills and building up a 'toolkit' which is then used to overcome OCD.

- Explain to your client that they will be very much in charge of the treatment, and they won't have to do anything they don't want to do.

HANDOUT: TREATMENT OVERVIEW

There is increasing evidence that psychological therapy called cognitive behaviour therapy (CBT) is an effective treatment for OCD.

What is CBT?

CBT helps by providing you with the tools necessary to manage your obsessions and compulsions. The most important part of CBT involves finding ways of going into situations that you find uncomfortable without engaging in rituals or compulsions.

What will my treatment involve?

Your CBT treatment will start with you having an opportunity to get to know your therapist and to ask any questions that you have. The main components of CBT include:

1. Setting goals that you would like to achieve.

2. Learning how OCD works.

3. Measuring the problem and repeating the measures at times.

4. Developing a set of techniques that you can use to start overcoming your OCD.

5. Putting your techniques into practice by completing behavioural tasks and challenges.

6. Developing strategies to make sure that you stay on top of your OCD into the longer term.

How long will my treatment last?

At the start of your treatment, your therapist will agree a number of meetings (sessions). They will review with you how treatment is progressing.

What will happen when my treatment ends?

At the end of your treatment, your therapist will discuss with you whether you have any further need for support.

Goal setting

From the outset, establish clearly what it is the client would like to achieve in terms of a reduction in OCD symptoms. Work collaboratively with your client to define these in clear, concrete and achievable terms. Try and collaborate to develop OCD SMART goals: Specific (to OCD), Measurable, Achievable, Realistic and Time-Limited. Write them down together on the goal-setting handout and each keep a copy (see Harold's completed goal-setting handout at the end of this section).

The person with OCD may be fearful about contemplating any change in very anxiety-provoking situations. Be sensitive to this, but suggest firmly that perhaps change in this area would be a very positive thing, and encourage your client to try and think about the idea of making change. However, if the person is resistant to this idea, identify goals with them that they feel are achievable and realistic. _If they have trouble identifying goals:_

If your client is having some problems identifying OCD-related goals, for example saying, 'Well, I need to do this that way', ask them _Q→_ what things they cannot do at present because of their rituals, worries and fears. Use this information to formulate treatment goals, for example 'To be able to reduce time in the bathroom in the morning to 30 minutes so that I can get to college on time.'

_²Q →_ It is also helpful at this stage to identify the things that the individual would like to do if they did not have OCD. This may be useful for motivation later in treatment.

Be aware that the OCD in itself may have additional functions for your client, such as keeping parents involved in their daily routine, helping them stay away from work or college settings where social interactions are very anxiety provoking. You can _Q→_ check this out by asking, 'If you did not have OCD, what would you do during the day?' And follow this up by asking, 'Would this cause _Q_ any stress or be difficult in any way?'

Where does OCD fall on list

This section may give you some more information about possible maintaining factors for the OCD. Remember, the autistic person has a lot to contend with, and they may perceive their OCD as a lesser problem. You can ask about this, perhaps by enquiring, *'If we made a list of all your problems or stresses and worries, would OCD be top of the list?'*

HANDOUT: GOAL SETTING (HAROLD)

By the end of my treatment I would like to achieve the following goals:

1. Spend 15 minutes in the morning having a shower and getting ready

2. Eat food cooked by other people.

Things I will be able to do if I achieve my treatment goals:

1. Be on time for college in the morning.

2. Go to a restaurant with Mum for her birthday.

3. Go to the Isle of Man TT race.

HANDOUT: GOAL SETTING

By the end of my treatment I would like to achieve the following goals:

1. _____

2. _____

3. _____

Things I will be able to do if I achieve my treatment goals:

1. _____

2. _____

3. _____

OCD psycho-education

1. what is OCD
2. Difference b/w obsession + compulsion
3. the maintaining nature of OCD cycle

It is important to ensure that the client gains a good understanding about what OCD is, the difference between obsessions and compulsions, and the maintaining nature of the OCD cycle. If your client has already had psychological treatment, they may have this knowledge but it is worth establishing what their understanding of their problems is. Use open questions first, and then if you need to, define the phenomena, and offer written definitions for the client to read outside the session.

OCD definitions

An obsession is a thought, image or impulse that keeps coming into a person's mind and is difficult to get rid of; for example, being afraid of dirt or germs, having thoughts and fears of harming someone else.

A compulsion is a feeling that a person has that they must repeat physical actions or mental acts. People with OCD may use these actions to help deal with an obsessive thought or 'neutralise' it; for example, excessive washing and cleaning, checking things repeatedly.

Emphasise the difference between obsessions and normal worries

Encourage the person to think of something that they are *worried about* (e.g., money, the weather, missing the bus) but not in an OCD way.

Think through with your client how these everyday worries differ from obsessions:

Normal		*Obsessions*
Usually based on facts or evidence	vs	Not based on facts or evidence
Tend to fade with facts or evidence	vs	Intrusive
Easier to 'switch on and off'	vs	Tend to get worse over time. The harder you try *not* to think about them, the more they come back.

Define what the word 'disorder' means

Clarify that the word 'disorder' simply means that the person has obsessions or compulsions to such an extent that they are interfering with the person's life.

Normalise obsessional thoughts

This is important for all individuals, but may be particularly pertinent for people with ASD who may not readily reflect on their thinking or have social networks and relationships that enable helpful conversations about unwanted thoughts.

Provide your client with a visual formulation of OCD

Once your client has developed a good understanding of what constitutes obsessions and compulsions, move on to providing them with a model of how they fit together and how this model might explain their problem.

The OCD cycle

This is a model that people with OCD tend to relate to easily. Alternatively called the 'OCD trap', it provides a simple but powerful representation of how one can become 'stuck' between anxiety and temporary relief. The OCD cycle can be used as an initial introductory model for all clients.

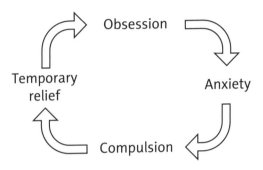

WORKSHEET: WHAT IS OCD?

O _____
_____
_____
_____

Examples:
_____
_____

C _____
_____
_____
_____

Examples:
_____
_____

D _____
_____
_____
_____

Examples:
_____
_____

HANDOUT: OCD DEFINITIONS

What is OCD?
Obsessive compulsive disorder (or OCD for short) is the name given to a condition in which a person has obsessions and/or compulsions, but usually both.

What is an obsession?
An obsession is a thought, image or impulse that keeps coming into a person's mind and is difficult to get rid of; for example, being afraid of dirt or germs, having thoughts and fears of harming someone else.

What is a compulsion?
A compulsion is a feeling that a person has that they must repeat physical actions or mental acts. People with OCD may use these actions to help deal with an obsessive thought or 'neutralise' it; for example, excessive washing and cleaning, checking things repeatedly.

HANDOUT: THE OCD TRAP

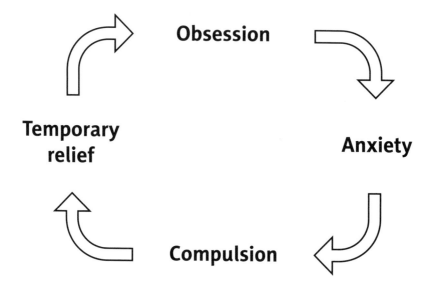

Obsession

Anxiety

Compulsion

Temporary relief

Formulation

A word about formulation. You will share a cross-sectional formulation of OCD with your client so they can understand how the problem works, and what is keeping it going. This might be as simple as the OCD cycle or trap depicted in the previous section.

You might want to develop a more elaborate formulation in collaboration with your client. This might include longitudinal factors that are important in the development of the OCD if your client wants to understand more about how the problem developed. We would recommend embarking on this in a comprehensive fashion, not just to understand the obsessions and compulsions, avoidance and safety behaviours, but because the likelihood of significant maintaining factors related to ASD are high. Your intervention will need at some level to address or take into account these maintaining factors and this is what sets apart adapted CBT from a straightforward, model-driven intervention.

The context (including the autism context) can be important in understanding the OCD. It can also signpost potential roadblocks on the path of treatment progress.

Consider the factors that are important in triggering and maintaining OCD in your individual client's case. Map these out using a diagram including obsessions, compulsions and avoidance behaviours. As an example, a formulation for Harold, our fictional client, is included at the end of this chapter.

Avoidance behaviours are those that reduce the individual's contact with feared stimuli. Examples include a person with contamination fears who avoids public toilets and a person with responsibility fears who avoids leaving the house because they would then need to check locks or windows. Such behaviours serve to maintain OCD by preventing the individual from confronting feared situations and discovering that (a) the feared outcome does not arise and (b) that they are able to cope with any associated worry or dysphoric feelings.

The context

Consider the context for the OCD. What is your individual's life-stage? What are their goals and progress with these? What other activities and routines are there in the person's daily life?

Are there any possible positive outcomes arising from the OCD? For example, does the individual also have marked social anxiety and avoid social situations? What will happen if they no longer have OCD?

- Will the day be empty?

- What will take the place of the OCD?

- Will they be expected to do more?

- What sorts of things might they be expected to do?

- How will this make them feel?

Possible maintaining factors might include:

- *Social anxiety:* Does the individual also feel anxious in social situations and does this anxiety prevent them from attending activities such as college or work? If yes, it is possible that social anxiety will be a maintaining factor in the OCD. The treatment plan might need to be informed by this issue.

- *High levels of ASD repetitive behaviours/Limited repertoire of adaptive behaviours:* You may need to take a 'ritual replacement' approach in addition to ERP. Even if the person stops the rituals, they will not readily replace them with a new behaviour. Suggest one, and if needed develop a 'menu' of alternative behaviours that are enjoyable, pleasurable, meaningful and easy to achieve so that in themselves they are reinforcing and anxiety reducing.

- *Executive function and daily living skill impairments:* It is always worth checking with the person, and their carer if possible, whether some of the time spent in self-care routines is a result of lacking the organisational and motor control skills to do these tasks in an efficient manner. It is also worth establishing what the person thinks 'most people do' in these situations. Your client may not have spent a lot of time with others to gain a sense of what is normal in the bathroom/shower and so on. If a clinical neuropsychological assessment is available, this may be useful. If this is not possible, a questionnaire measure about behavioural aspects of executive function may be a useful tool.

- *Lack of access to meaningful and constructive daily routine/ Concerns about the future:* These are applicable to all autistic people, but particularly to young people at transition points. Leaving school and attending college (less structured, more socially demanding) can result in increased anxiety levels and the tendency to manage this with rituals and other methods can increase. Perfectionism and routines around homework are not uncommon. Awareness of difference and lack of clarity around the path to independence as a young adult can be huge issues. These are concomitant problems of ASD but may have a central role in the onset or maintenance of the obsessional complaints.

Cognitive component

We are taking a behavioural approach to understanding and intervening with OCD. This is in line with the evidence base for OCD treatment as well as the recommended adaptations to CBT for autism.

However, it can be helpful to understand the personal meaning and beliefs relevant to the OCD formulation in individual cases. Here, the clinician assists the client to discover the thoughts, interpretations and underlying beliefs involved in the maintenance of OCD. While this is generally done in a 'here and now' fashion, reference can be made to how automatic thoughts may have been influenced by earlier childhood events or experiences. Common cognitive elements to an OCD formulation include the client's inflated sense of responsibility, an over-importance placed on certain thoughts, a belief that thoughts equal reality, an over-estimation of the likelihood of catastrophic events, and an intolerance of uncertainties or imperfection. For example, thoughts about harming a family member might lead an individual to believe that they must be a bad person who wants to hurt their family because they have this thought. They may be taking a number of other measures to counteract this belief, they may have lost self-confidence and all esteem because of this belief, and some skill building and esteem bolstering work may be needed.

Therapist tips

- You may want to involve parents, partners or professional carers and support workers in some of the treatment sessions. Support from family members and carers and education of significant others about OCD and the treatment programme may be particularly important for autistic people and aid generalisation.

- Ensure your client has a good grasp of their OCD cycle.

- Remember that you may need to spend longer on this part of treatment than you would for a person without autism.

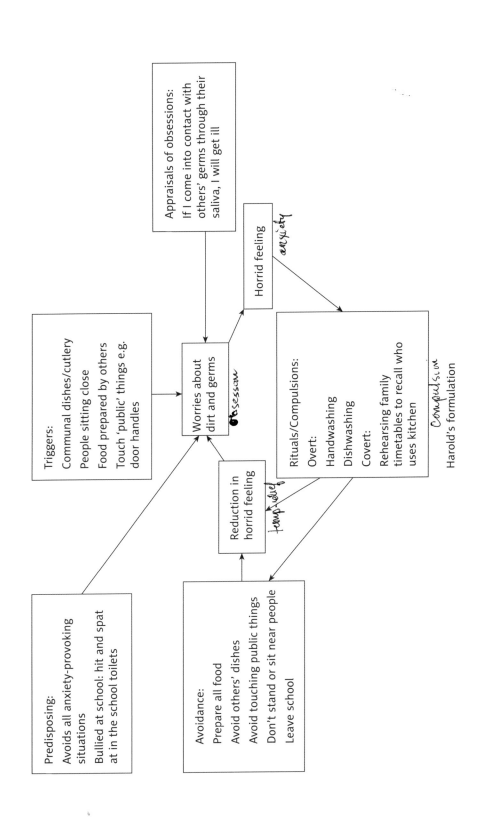

Predisposing:
Avoids all anxiety-provoking situations
Bullied at school: hit and spat at in the school toilets

Triggers:
Communal dishes/cutlery
People sitting close
Food prepared by others
Touch 'public' things e.g. door handles

Appraisals of obsessions:
If I come into contact with others' germs through their saliva, I will get ill

Worries about dirt and germs

Obsession

Horrid feeling

anxiety

Rituals/Compulsions:
Overt:
Handwashing
Dishwashing
Covert:
Rehearsing family timetables to recall who uses kitchen

Compulsion

Reduction in horrid feeling

temporal

Avoidance:
Prepare all food
Avoid others' dishes
Avoid touching public things
Don't stand or sit near people
Leave school

Harold's formulation

Chapter 4

CBT PHASE 2 UNDERSTANDING AND RATING ANXIETY

Agenda

- Rationale

- Key considerations

- Understanding anxiety

- Noticing and rating anxiety

- Anxiety management/relaxation

- Anxiety and exposure and response prevention

Rationale

Helping your client to develop an understanding of anxiety and establish a system to measure and monitor anxiety are some of the key challenges.

A good understanding of anxiety may take a little time and creativity on your part, but if you and your client work together this is usually something that can be achieved in a session.

A valid, often idiosyncratic, anxiety rating system will help you and your client to identify increasingly difficult exposure tasks and ultimately map out a fear hierarchy. It will also enable your client to start practising noticing subtle changes in their anxiety levels, particularly if they tend to experience emotions as 'all or nothing' – something which is commonly reported by autistic people. This will increase the chances of your client fully engaging with exposure and response prevention and being able to monitor their anxiety as it dissipates over time.

The aim is to make the abstract concept of degree, quality or quantity of anxiety into a concrete and tangible representation.

Key considerations

Autistic people will vary in terms of their ability to recognise and rate their anxiety. Some may arrive with their own way of communicating how anxious they are, others may relate quickly and easily to the traditional 0–10 system. Most people may need time to develop an individualised system that 'fits'.

Recognising, labelling and expressing emotions can be different in autistic people. They might use different words or concepts to describe how they are feeling. They might struggle to notice feelings, or interpret them accurately. If you have become aware of this during the assessment phase, it will be important to include at least one educational session about anxiety in the early stages of treatment, and certainly before any exposure-based activities begin.

Your client will need time to learn about anxiety and often they may need a session in understanding how anxiety differs from other emotions, what it may feel like, and why we have it.

Understanding anxiety

You are probably very used to discussing what 'anxiety' is, and how and why humans experience such an emotion.

Ask your client what 'anxiety' (or preferred term) means to them and where it comes from. Have a general discussion about anxiety. Use the body map you generated during the assessment phase to talk about the physical aspects of anxiety.

It is important that you include the client's own symptoms of anxiety. For example, if your client reports physical anxiety symptoms in their stomach, explain how this is the result of blood being diverted from digesting food to the large muscle groups in our arms and legs. If you did not make a body map of anxiety symptoms before, this is a good time to do so.

The range of physical symptoms of anxiety, tension and stress can be reviewed, and includes:

- tense muscles (e.g., a stiff neck, back or headache)

- slowed digestion (e.g., upset stomach or butterflies)

- fast heart rate (e.g., blushing, pounding heart or 'skipped' beats)

- increased sweating

- faster breathing.

Explain that anxiety is an unpleasant feeling of tension, a sense that something negative, unwanted or threatening is about to occur. It can be persistent and pervasive. It is a feeling state very closely related to fear. Fear is an emotional reaction to a specific, perceived physical or psychological danger. A fear reaction can be intense and useful in an emergency. The fear response is sometimes termed the 'fight or flight' response. It is an acute stress response, evolved to be adaptive and functional, and designed to assist us to fight for our lives or flee to safety when we are in danger. There are some species where 'freezing' is part of adaptive responding when under threat. Although the fear response is unpleasant, people sometimes seek out this response on theme park rides or other high-adrenaline activities.

During the 'fight or flight' response, a range of physiological changes takes place in our bodies to help us survive. These include changes in our chemistry and changes in our blood flow, designed to direct blood towards our muscles and limbs and prepare us for action. It is a good idea to have a body map showing these changes. These are generally available from websites, textbooks or anxiety self-help resources. You may have versions that you use routinely in your clinical practice. You can relate this to your client's own body map to see how their symptoms of anxiety fit with the normal human fear response.

Explain that our bodies have evolved to help us survive in perilous conditions. Although we continue to face peril, this has reduced dramatically in the modern world. However, we continue to have an acute stress response system that leaps into action when we perceive danger. Our fear reaction can become 'misplaced' and we can have a strong response to situations we have become afraid of and worried about, but which don't necessarily present as dangerous.

Fear is usually a response to a specific threat and can be time-limited and 'episodic'. However, anxiety can also be in the background a lot of the time. We can be in a state of anxious tension, anticipating uncertain danger and threat. It can be hard sometimes to distinguish between the two emotions. An episode of fear usually leaves a person feeling very anxious for a while. The physiological symptoms of both states are similar. People often use the terms interchangeably.

Discuss how anxiety and fear are different from other emotions. Use the types of handouts and materials you would ordinarily use with clients for these areas.

Notice the kinds of questions or comments your client makes. Ask them to summarise the explanation. Ask them if this fits with their understanding of fear and anxiety.

If your client struggles to relate to the description and definition of anxiety, you may need to use your client's special interest or another topic as a concrete analogy to help aid understanding. We explain how to do this in the next section.

Noticing and rating anxiety

Here your task as therapist is to socialise your client to the notion that anxiety is not an 'all or nothing' phenomenon. There are situations where the response is rapid and extreme, but, generally, anxiety and the stress response range from low-level 'anxious discomfort' to top of the scale 'fear', with several stages in between.

One area of difficulty can be identifying the varying degrees of an emotion such as anxiety. This will require support from you as the therapist. You might be able to use the sorts of informational resources you use with all your clients. The adaptations outlined below are suggestions for when the usual material does not seem to be accessible and there are some ideas to help your client develop an understanding of varying degrees of anxiety, for example using special interests, concrete examples or varying degrees of physical symptoms as a way to understand this.

When assisting your client to develop an anxiety rating system, you may find it helpful to:

- try using a system of colours, with or without numbers, rather than numbers alone

- experiment with various approaches until your client finds one that 'fits'

- use your client's own words for their experiences rather than sticking with traditional CBT terms such as 'SUDS' (Subjective Units of Distress Scale) or 'anxiety thermometer'

- encourage the use of analogy where appropriate, with reference to the client's area of special interest

- use concrete examples of non-OCD anxiety-provoking situations to anchor the scale

- use intensity or frequency of different physical symptoms (such as heart rate) to help your client understand different degrees of the emotion.

If needed, use behavioural exposure with a non-OCD stimulus to provoke mild anxiety to help the client notice how they feel when they are anxious.

Introduce your client to the notion of rating anxiety

To start this session, introduce your client to the idea that learning about and rating their anxiety will help them learn about how their OCD works.

> T: *In today's session, we are going to focus a bit more on your anxiety. We are going to see if we can figure out a way of measuring whether you are just a little bit anxious or really, really anxious in a specific situation.*

Provide a non-OCD example of how anxiety varies in intensity

Assist your client to see that everyone tends to feel different levels of anxiety in different situations. Where possible, suggest that your client thinks about a non-OCD experience that makes them feel anxious – heights is a good example:

> T: *Imagine for a second that you are scared of heights. Think for a second about how it feels to jump out of an aeroplane. Do you think you would feel anxious?*
>
> C: *Yes, very. I don't think I'd ever do it.*
>
> T: *Now, think about how you would feel on the London Eye when it turns around and you are right at the top. Do you think that you would feel more or less anxious than in the aeroplane?*
>
> C: *Less. But I wouldn't go on the London Eye.*
>
> T: *Ok. How about standing at the top of the stairs? Would you be more anxious in the aeroplane example or more anxious standing at the top of the stairs...?*

You can also use examples of different situations which cause different levels of anxiety to illustrate the same point.

For instance, with one client, examples of different situations causing anxiety were put on sticky notes and then a session was spent putting them in order of which made the client more anxious and less anxious, to illustrate not all situations cause the same level of anxiety. Questions such as *'Do you feel more anxious when you go to the shops or when you are at home?'* were used to arrange the sticky notes. This approach also helps keep this discussion embedded in concrete examples, which is more helpful and more appealing to this client group. You can also use distance between the sticky notes to help indicate the differences in the degree of emotion.

Discuss how anxiety can vary in intensity

With some clients, you may be able to think of a way to use their special interest to illustrate degrees of anxiety. It is important that this is a shared endeavour, and the ideas and knowledge come from the client. Do not try to 'force' their special interest into this. It should happen easily and come from the client primarily. We illustrate this with Harold later in the chapter.

Use the body map

Some clients may prefer reference to the varying degrees of behavioural or physiological cues of anxiety as a way to understand the varying degrees of it. If you have not already completed a body map of anxiety symptoms, it is a good idea to do it at this point (see Chapter 2). With your client, identify what physical symptoms they experience when feeling anxious. It may be helpful for them to relate it to something they are very scared of in order to elicit the experience, or if they cannot do this, use real or imaginal exposure to trigger these symptoms. It may be helpful to have a list of the most common symptoms of anxiety for the client to choose from. Go through the body and ask them how they feel, for example, *'When you were there, was your heart racing? Were you sweating?'* You can use the diagram of the body to illustrate where they may notice different symptoms of anxiety, and colours to represent different levels of intensity, for example red when all symptoms are at their highest, green when calmer. It is useful to ask questions such as,

'When your heart races when you're anxious, do you sometimes notice it races faster in some situations and less so in others?' It may be helpful to pick two or three of the most noticeable signs in doing this. This can help the client to develop an understanding of there being different degrees of anxiety.

Introduce the notion of rating anxiety

Discuss with your client the usefulness of a system for rating anxiety.

> T: *Next, we are going to work on developing a system for keeping track of how anxious you are feeling. There are a lot of different ways of doing this and it is important that we choose a way that fits for you.*

Review rating scale options

Provide your client with some examples of rating systems used by other people with autism spectrum disorders.

Traditional 0–10

Some people with ASD may be perfectly comfortable using a 0–10 or 0–100 rating scale system. If this needs scaffolding, you could support it with a visual image such as a thermometer. However, some people may associate this with rising anger.

Graphic scales

Some people may like the idea of numbers representing different degrees of discomfort or anxiety, but might find it a bit too abstract and like an accompanying visual aid. For example, boxes increasing in size along a line might be a useful visual cue to accompany the numbers.

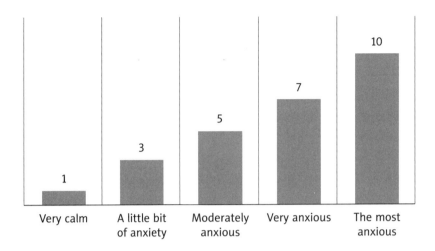

Ten choices might be appropriate for some while others might prefer just three or four. Numbers representing the magnitude or intensity of the emotion may or may not be helpful.

The boxes can be coloured or left blank. If coloured, it can be helpful to use light to darker shades as the emotional intensity increases. The colour charts available in paint shops can be helpful as a resource. The colour should be the client's choice, which they feel fits with their internal experience of anxiety. We are showing it in monochrome here.

Most anxious
Very anxious
Moderately anxious
A little bit anxious
Mild

Some people relate well to a 'traffic lights' system for rating anxiety. They feel more comfortable with three choices, and relate better to changes in colour rather than numbers to rate the intensity of their anxiety – thus green becomes calm, ascending to amber when things are feeling more uncomfortable and finally to red when anxiety or discomfort is at its worst.

Practise using the rating scale with your client

Once you and your client have developed a rating scale for anxiety or discomfort that seems to fit with their experiences, and which they can use, encourage them to practise with it.

Start by trying to anchor the lower extremity of the scale. Prompt your client to think of situations when they feel calm, such as when they are resting, watching television or engaged in an activity they enjoy and find absorbing.

> T: *Let's think about what the 'green' zone on the traffic lights feels like. Can you think of a time when you felt calm and relaxed, in the green zone?*
>
> C: *I'm not sure.*
>
> T: *What about when you are looking at your pictures of fungi? Do you think you might be in the green zone then?*
>
> C: *I think so.*
>
> T: *Great, and how does your body feel when you are in the green zone?*

Next, help your client to anchor the upper extremity of the scale using a non-OCD example of an anxiety-provoking situation. An activity such as skydiving can be a useful example. Prompt your client to think about the upper extremity of the scale, to be reserved for extremely anxiety-provoking (virtually life or death) situations.

Finally, assist your client to find a point on the scale which matches their anxiety levels while they are talking to you in the session. Many autistic people report their baseline levels to be around 3/10 on a 0–10 scale. They may never really feel less than this.

Ask your client about their current physiological state and if they notice any bodily sensations that would help to anchor that number on the scale. You can ask what their heartbeat is like, where they notice any other bodily sensations, what word they would use to describe how they are feeling right now. If your client struggles with this, wearable health devices such as a simple heart-rate monitor, often used by runners, can help your client by making the biofeedback links direct and explicit.

Anxiety management/relaxation

Your client may not have good anxiety management skills. Relaxation training may be an important component of education about anxiety, so that the individual learns more about the emotion. Standard relaxation scripts and tapes can be used, but autistic people may need more time and attention to learn the techniques. We have found two or three sessions can sometimes be necessary to grasp the method of diaphragmatic breathing, for example. Generally, relaxation is best taught by therapist instruction in sessions with good therapist observation to notice and correct any problems. Individualised scripts and tapes using preferred imagery or sounds can be very useful. If an anxiety management group is available as an adjunct to individual CBT, this is of great benefit.

Harold and the motorbike

Harold is a young man with a diagnosis of autism spectrum disorder. He attends college part time and lives at home with his family. Harold is very interested in motorbikes. He has liked them since he was young. He has many motorbike magazines; he has a motorbike he likes to fix up and improve, and eventually he would like to work as a motorbike mechanic.

When we introduced Harold, we mentioned that he is particularly concerned about germs and dirt. He worries that others' saliva might touch him and make him ill, so he avoids being close to people. He will not eat food that others have prepared and will only eat food that has been packaged and sealed in a factory environment. He washes his own dishes, won't put his clothes in a communal family laundry and carries wipes around to clean door handles. He avoids washing as the accompanying rituals and measures to prevent contamination mean that a simple shower can take four hours. Harold is aware that this is not usual, but struggles to resist the worries and compulsions, saying, *'It is the way it is, there are germs everywhere and I need to make sure I don't get ill.'*

Harold is not very good at noticing and labelling emotions. He can get very cross and upset when his family try to encourage him to eat with them or sit and watch TV on the couch. When Harold attended for assessment, the therapist discussed how he felt when thoughts about germs came into his mind. Harold described needing to wash, having to 'run away' from the situation but was not able to describe how it felt inside.

The therapist and Harold completed a body map and the therapist was clear that this probably was anxiety. Harold used the word *'horrible'* for the feeling.

The therapist tried to explain how these feelings in his body and the 'horrible' worry were anxiety, an emotion. Harold struggled with this explanation and continued to externalise or be objective about his feelings, *'It just happens, horrible just happens and then I have to wash.'* The therapist used a factsheet about anxiety and the evolutionary explanation for why humans experience this emotional state. Harold could not relate to this.

The therapist wondered about motorbikes, and whether motorbikes were always the same, always running smoothly. Harold explained this was not the case, that motorbikes have a system where fuel and air combines, is ignited and the resulting 'explosion' pushes the pistons up and down to make the engine run. If the fuel mixture is wrong, or the engine is being revved too much, the engine can get too hot, then the engine can splutter, backfire, vibrate excessively and even stop running altogether. Harold explained that, for example, if the air filter were dirty it would lead to a shortage of air in the fuel/air mixture and the bike might run too hot. Or, when the engine is running too fast and the gear is not altered, the engine can overheat. The therapist wondered if this might be a helpful and concrete analogy to explain what happens when people get anxious. People are a system like motorbikes, and if something changes in the system so that a neurochemical like adrenaline surges, the system can splutter, backfire and not run smoothly.

Harold began to relate more to the idea that there are things that might affect the human system which are internal. This allowed the therapist and Harold to discuss how emotions are a good barometer of the system.

Harold also enjoyed talking about motorbikes to the therapist, and was quite excited to use his interest as part of the anxiety rating scale. He understood clearly that there were different phases of a motorbike engine running more or less smoothly, and this enabled the therapist to explain that the same thing happened with the human systems.

Together they made a motorbike rating scale and mapped Harold's human system alongside to represent his system not running smoothly, when the feeling was 'horrible'. It allowed them to think about the different phases of this system running more or less smoothly. They were able to identify three feeling states which Harold could relate to different OCD situations.

The therapist asked Harold to practise using the rating scale as homework between sessions, noticing the different phases. He was encouraged to add more detail to this if needed.

Harold's motorbike rating scale

Engine revs increased
Check the dial
Really need to change gear
Engine far too hot
Pistons firing up and down
at full speed
Everything shaking

High revs in engine
No gear change
Engine getting hotter
Pistons going up and down
more quickly
Vibrations on the bike
increase

Engine smooth
running
Purring gently
Low revs
Engine quite cool

Harold's motorbike rating scale

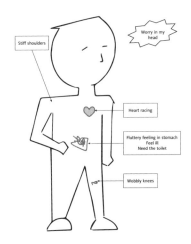

Most horrible feeling 10/10
Really worried about germs
Can't touch
Heart racing ++
Stomach feels ill

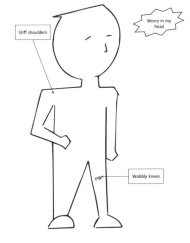

A bit horrible 6/10
Feel wobbly in knees
Stiff shoulders
Worry in head

System calm 2/10
No OCD worries
Feel smooth
Driving along a quiet road

Harold's OCD rating scale

Anxiety and exposure and response prevention

By now, your client should be able to notice and rate different 'shades' of anxiety. They will have foundation knowledge about the nature of anxiety. You will have a shared way to communicate about this emotional state.

If this is the case, it is time to move on to discussing the rationale for the treatment model for OCD, i.e. exposure and response prevention.

Exposure and response prevention (ERP) is recommended as the most effective psychological treatment for OCD (NICE 2005). The principles of ERP comprise an individual confronting an OCD trigger (exposure) while resisting any urges to engage in neutralising or compulsive behaviour (response prevention). Within a purely behavioural framework, ERP results in the extinction of anxiety in response to the trigger. In a more cognitive behavioural framework, ERP assists in the process of identifying and modifying distorted cognitions about the risks associated with various behaviours or stimuli. The bulk of any CBT intervention for OCD should be devoted to supporting your client to engage in regular ERP tasks. It is important that these tasks are carried out within sessions, but also as homework. In fact, ERP carried out regularly for homework is the single best predictor of improvement in adult trials (Simpson *et al.* 2012).

A good understanding of the rationale behind ERP is essential so your client is fully informed and accepting of the treatment model. It can seem counter-intuitive to deliberately enter situations that you avoid because they make you feel anxious.

By now, you as a therapist will be used to using visual aids to explain psychological concepts, and this is particularly important here – do not rely on verbal explanations alone. You will need paper and pen(s).

Begin by explaining that it is now time to start talking about anxiety and OCD. You might say something along the lines of:

> T: *When we have been rating and learning about anxiety, I think we both agree that although it is a normal part of human experience that*

can be helpful to us in certain situations as a cue and mechanism to respond to danger, it can be an unpleasant experience. So let's take a look at exactly what happens to your anxiety levels when you are in an OCD situation.

Discuss and draw out what happens to your client's anxiety when they engage in compulsions. Ask your client what happens to anxiety when they are in a situation where OCD is triggered.

Let's use Harold as an example.

T: *Harold, did anything happen today to trigger a difficult OCD situation and the horrid feeling?*

Harold: *Yes, I was trying to make my breakfast and none of my plates were in the cupboard.*

T: *Tell me a bit more about your plates.*

Harold: *I have my own plates and cutlery, and I wash them myself in boiling water with anti-bacterial solution. They don't go in the dishwasher. This morning, someone had used my plates and knife. They were in the dishwasher that had just finished. I wanted to eat some toast before I came here. I didn't have time to clean and prepare the sink to wash my dishes. I had to rinse and rinse the plate and knife with the water from the kettle before I used them.*

T: *Ok, thank you for explaining that. So what happened to the horrid feeling when you saw your dishes in the dishwasher and knew someone had used them?*

Harold: *It was strong.*

T: *How strong, on our motorbike scale, what number would you put on it?*

Harold: *About 7/10 or 8/10. Very strong.*

T: *Ok, let's put that on this chart here as 8. Once you washed the plates with the boiled water, what happened to the horrid feeling?*

Harold: *It went down, to about 2. I knew they were clean but it still did not feel great.*

T: *Ok, let's put about 2 on the chart, so the horrid feeling came down. Did anything else happen before you left the house that triggered your OCD?*

Harold: *Yes, I was late because of washing the plates, and I was hurrying to leave the house. I couldn't go upstairs and find the wipes. I was frightened about opening the front door.*

T: *Ok, so how did that feel? Can we put a number on it?*

Harold: *Horrid, about 7/10.*

T: *What did you do?*

Harold: *I pulled down my sleeve to cover my hand and opened the door that way. Then when I got to the garage to get my motorbike, I knew there were spare wipes there and I could clean my hands.*

T: *What happened to the horrid feeling?*

Harold: *Well it went down a bit because I did not have to touch the door handle and I could clean my hands in the garage.*

T: *Just using this morning as an example, it seems that when OCD is triggered, you do a compulsion such as washing the plate in very hot water or washing your hands. This makes you feel better and the anxiety comes down, but before you know it, something else causes you to start to worry again. Your anxiety shoots up, you do compulsions and it comes down again. If we map out the anxiety or horrid feeling on the chart, it goes up and down, up and down. It looks exhausting. Is this how it is for you?*

Harold: *Yes, like a roller coaster.*

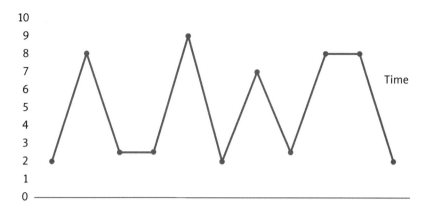

Anxiety before and after compulsions

What happens to anxiety when you don't do compulsions?

Once you have established the pattern of anxiety that occurs when your client does compulsions, have a discussion to try and predict what will happen if they don't.

T: *I am wondering what you think would happen to your anxiety if you did not do the compulsions, if you resisted the urge to wash your hands?*

Harold: *Well, I would feel horrid and need to wash my hands, what else?*

T: *Sometimes people worry that if they do not do the compulsion, the anxiety feelings will last forever. Or they worry that they might go mad or have a heart attack or something because of the anxiety. Do you worry about these things?*

Harold: *Well yes, it feels like I am going crazy when the horrid feeling is strong.*

T: *Looking at our diagram of anxiety and compulsions, I wonder what you think would happen over time?*

Harold: *What do you mean?*

T: *Well, imagine that your heart is racing and racing and keeps on racing. What will happen to it eventually?*

Harold: *I guess it will give up, either collapse or slow down.*

T: *Right, it won't be able to keep up that racing pace. No matter how anxious you get, the feeling will always pass with time. This happens because most of the changes that take place in our bodies during the fight or flight response can only be kept up for a little while. Then our bodies get exhausted and have to slow back down. So let's look at the graph and see what happens to the anxiety (horrid feeling) if you don't do the compulsions. It will go up, and then come down; it might take some time, but it will come down again.*

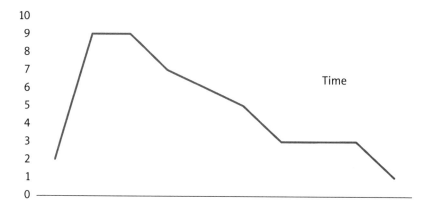

Anxiety when you resist compulsions

Why does anxiety reduce over time?

You might need to spend a bit of time with your client, reviewing how anxiety comes down over time. You can refer again to the changes that happen with the fight or flight response being temporary.

You could draw on your client's own experience. Help your client remember a time when they felt anxious, but the anxiety passed without them doing a compulsion. It might be easiest to first think of a non-OCD situation.

T: *Harold, I am wondering if you can think of a time when you felt really anxious but the anxiety passed.*

Harold: *Not really.*

T: *How about going to college? I remember when you told me about the first few days at college you said you used to feel very scared going into the classroom.*

Harold: *Yeah, well there were all these people there and I did not know what to expect.*

T: *Ok, so what happened?*

Harold: *The first day was awful, and I thought I couldn't cope. I sat at the back and I felt terrified. Then we had a workshop session and we got to take apart an engine, and it was sort of fun. Me and another guy were talking about the exhaust and that was easy. I started to feel more relaxed, and it got easier to go back into the classroom.*

T: *Ok, so at first you were really scared but you went into the classroom anyway.*

Harold: *Yeah.*

T: *And you stayed for the whole first day?*

Harold: *Yes.*

T: *So what happened to the scared feeling during the course of that first day?*

Harold: *It was terrible and I guess it got a bit better as the day went on.*

T: *Do you think you got used to it?*

Harold: *Yes, and the engine workshop was fun.*

T: *So it seems that if we drew out the anxiety when you started college, it might start out high in the morning, but over the day it got a bit lower, and then when you did the engine workshop it reduced more. So the scared feeling went away over time.*

Introduce the notion of repeated exposure

Once the client is familiar with the idea that anxiety passes over time and can relate that to their own experience, prompt them to talk about what might happen if they confronted the same feared stimulus or situation, over and over again.

T: *So you were telling me how scared you felt on the first day of college. Is that the first time that happened to you?*

Harold: *No, I was really scared every day when I went to school.*

T: *Right, so it was pretty hard to start in a new college. I am wondering what would happen if you had to start another course today?*

Harold: *Well, I wouldn't like it, but if it was about an interesting engine thing, I would feel scared but not too scared.*

T: *So not as scared as before when you went to school, or when you started college?*

Harold: *Yes, I might be a bit less scared the next time.*

T: *And what do you think would happen if you started a new engine course next week, and then another new one the week after?*

Harold: *I guess each time it might get a bit easier. Depends on the people and if there are bullies there, but otherwise might be ok.*

You can draw out with your client what happens to anxiety in a situation when you repeatedly enter it.

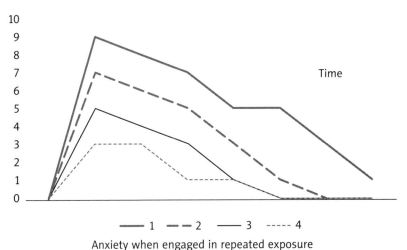

Anxiety when engaged in repeated exposure

Introduce the notion of exposure and response prevention (ERP)

This idea of anxiety extinguishing over repeated episodes of exposure to the feared situation is the foundation of behavioural approaches to treating OCD.

Emphasise to the client that this is what you will be doing over coming sessions.

> T: *This process of facing the things we fear is one of the key elements of CBT approaches to treating OCD. In a careful and planned manner, we are going to start talking about you entering situations or tasks that trigger OCD, getting anxious, and not doing compulsions. We should find that if you do this repeatedly, and don't do the compulsions, your anxiety will pass and in fact each time you go into the situation or come into contact with the OCD trigger, the anxiety will be less. This process is called exposure and response prevention or ERP. The important thing about ERP is that you will be in charge. There won't be any surprises. This is your treatment and you won't have to do anything that you do not think will be helpful or you don't feel able to do.*

Plan on purpose = control

If your client is very unsure about the model for treatment, you can suggest a trial with an anxiety trigger not related to the OCD, and which is not too anxiety provoking. They can track anxiety on a graph with repeated exposure to see if their experience is consistent with the ERP model. This may help with education about anxiety and improve confidence in the treatment model.

By now you and your client ideally should be confident that the following issues have been addressed and the building blocks for CBT are in place:

Teaching

- What are obsessions and compulsions?

- What is anxiety and why do we have it?

- What is your client's individual experience of anxiety?

- How do we notice and measure different intensities of anxiety?

- What role does anxiety play in OCD?

- How can behaving differently when OCD is triggered help change the problem of OCD?

Chapter 5

CBT PHASE 2 EXPOSURE AND RESPONSE PREVENTION

Agenda

- Key considerations
- Creating a hierarchy
- Carrying out ERP tasks
- Generalising: spreading and sharing the gains
- Therapist tips

Key considerations

- Taking a more therapist-directed approach in generating the hierarchy and planning exposure and homework tasks.

- Grading the hierarchy subtly to help introduce change, particularly in the early stages to increase confidence and the likelihood of success.

- Distinguishing between subtle grading or steps to generate a realistic hierarchy which will not feel overwhelming, but which sufficiently facilitates ERP.

- Ensuring the hierarchy steps are operationalised as clear, concrete and specific.

- Undertaking in vivo work with therapist modelling.

- Navigating roadblocks, such as those caused by an intense experience of anxiety.

- Distinguishing between avoidance of situations due to OCD and avoidance related to other factors.

Creating a hierarchy

The purpose of a fear or exposure hierarchy is to develop a list of perceived challenges and put them in order of difficulty from least to most distressing or challenging.

The list should include situations or objects that trigger the urge to engage in compulsions. It should also include situations or objects the individual currently avoids because they elicit anxiety or OCD symptoms.

The hierarchy provides a framework, or map, of how the client will confront fears in a staged and predictable fashion where mastery at one level increases confidence in being able to proceed to higher levels.

Many clients with ASD may struggle with this as they may have difficulty in ranking items, they may see things in an 'all or nothing' way or they may struggle to generate a list of triggers at all. There are various ways to overcome these issues and we discuss them below.

We recommend you spend a whole session developing a hierarchy. Steps to creating a hierarchy include assisting your client to generate a list of feared situations or stimuli and helping them to place these in order of difficulty, ideally with a relatively even spread across easier to harder tasks.

Introduce concept of hierarchy to client

The first step in developing a hierarchy with the client is to provide them with a rationale. This is how it was explained to Harold:

T: *Today we are going to start mapping out a series of tasks or challenges that are going to help you to overcome your OCD. We will start by thinking of some tasks that you find relatively easy to do before moving on to some more difficult tasks.*

It can be useful at this point to provide your client with a pictorial representation of the purpose of an exposure hierarchy. For example, the diagram below can prompt your client to think about someone confronted by an apparently insurmountable obstacle. Personalise the scenario by encouraging the client to imagine that at the top of the obstacle is a desired object (related to the client's special interest if appropriate). Harold was given the following explanation along with the picture.

T: *Imagine this is you, standing here on the ground. In front of you is this high wall. At the top of the building is bag with £1000 in it. What do you think you would spend the money on if you could reach it?*

Harold: *A new computer.*

T: *Sounds good. You were telling me earlier how you'd really like to get a new computer. We have a problem though, don't we? Here's you down here and there's your cash at the top of the wall. What do you think would happen if you tried to reach it from there?*

Harold: *I couldn't.*

T: *Probably not. So any ideas? How are we going to get you to the top of the wall?*

Harold: *I could use a ladder?*

Using the diagram, illustrate the advantages of a step-by-step or ladder approach:

£1000

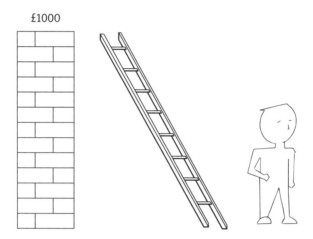

The ultimate goal may seem unattainable from where they are standing at present, but the very first step may feel just within reach. Once this first step has been attained, the next step might then feel just possible and so on up the ladder. Each successful step leads to a sense of progress and increased confidence, and all the time, the goal is getting closer.

Relate the concept of a hierarchy to OCD

Suggest to your client that this same process is relevant for overcoming OCD; for example, this is how it was explained to Harold:

T: *Just like in the diagram, right now the prospect of using a public toilet without washing your hands might feel virtually impossible, would you agree?*

Harold: *Yes, completely.*

T: *But what about the prospect of standing outside a public toilet but not going in? Or using a public toilet just after it has been cleaned?*

Harold: *I'd have to spend time checking that it had been cleaned properly; that would take ages, but I could stand outside the public toilet while waiting.*

T: *And that's what people often find. One challenge might seem just a tiny bit less difficult than another – just a tiny bit more achievable.*

Provide a framework for the hierarchy

Before starting work on the hierarchy, refresh your client's memory of the anxiety rating system that you developed earlier in treatment. Check that your client still finds it relevant and it still 'fits' with their experience of anxiety and OCD. If not, then spend time refining this system before moving on.

Next, try and 'anchor' the rating system by thinking of extreme scenarios that fit with the highest and lowest values on the rating system. If your client is feeling anxious, try starting with the lowest value on their rating scale. This rating is reserved for times that they feel completely calm. Help your client to think of examples such as when they are watching television, reading a book or engaging in a special interest. Prompt your client to think about the physical sensations that fit with those behaviours. How is their body feeling? What is the word that describes how they are feeling? Make use of the body map here, if your client finds this helpful.

Finally, move on to anchoring the top end of the scale. This is reserved for the most anxiety-provoking situations – virtual 'life or death' scenarios. Being explicit about what fits at this end of the hierarchy will help your client to avoid the temptation of labelling every exposure task at the maximum end of the scale. It is sometimes helpful to start with non-OCD scenarios such as skydiving or being attacked by a lion before moving on to OCD-related situations if your client is struggling.

Brainstorming and starting to generate a hierarchy

It may be difficult for autistic people to generate ideas for the hierarchy but it is important that they feel engaged and collaborate in this process. If this is the case for your client, here are some ideas that you could use:

- List all the compulsions OCD 'makes me do' and then take each compulsion in turn, listing common triggers.

- Ask your client to refer to their list of goals; take each goal and list the OCD symptoms and the triggers that they need to overcome to reach their goal. This might be a useful way of keeping it concrete for your client. Additionally, embedding ERP within a desired goal framework may help to maintain motivation when you come to completing ERP tasks.

- If there is a range of obsessive and compulsive symptoms across different domains (e.g., harm obsessions and con-tamination obsessions), it will probably be helpful to begin with a focus on a single symptom domain (perhaps the area that causes slightly less distress) and then move on to others sequentially. This may make things feel more contained and manageable for your client.

- If the OCD symptoms are quite abstract (e.g., a worry that you might inadvertently do something wrong), the impact on daily function can be pervasive. It can be helpful to begin by developing a circumscribed hierarchy, for example a particular checking routine or ritual. This will make the treatment approach concrete for your client and present a good starting point from which early success can expand to develop hierarchies for additional situations and rituals.

- A graded approach is extremely important. It is far better for things to have early success no matter how 'gentle' than for your client to feel overwhelmed by intensely anxious experiences or problems completing the tasks.

Whatever the method of generating the list, remember to include triggers that OCD makes the client avoid. It is important to disentangle avoidance attributable to the core features of autism from avoidance behaviours driven by OCD. For example, there may be a restricted range of places and activities due to social difficulties or lack of opportunities, as well as restrictions related to OCD. Therefore, it is important to make sure that in the hierarchy you keep a focus on OCD-driven avoidance for later ERP tasks. However, in doing so you may need to consider whether there is other support you can put in place targeted at skill building and providing access to social, educational and occupational activities. This may involve facilitating access to support in order to manage difficulties related to autism.

Another area to include when generating a hierarchy is what OCD 'makes other people do', for example give reassurance. You can refer to the Family Accommodation Scale if you have completed this with a family member or carer at the start of treatment.

It is often helpful to ask a family member to join for part of these sessions to ensure that all areas are covered if your client consents to this. Do not forget to ask about any hidden or covert rituals, and put them on the list. This could include praying or cancelling bad thoughts in their head. Remember that some autistic people have difficulties with Theory of Mind and therefore may assume that you know about their thoughts and experiences without being explicitly told. As a therapist, hold in mind that the goal is not to get an exhaustive list of every symptom but a range, so that a hierarchy can be put together. Some austistic people may struggle with not making a long and exhaustive list, so you may wish to develop some rules around this such as putting a limit on the number of items on the hierarchy or a rule of how many symptoms to write for each OCD dimension. You can give the rationale that it cannot all be tackled in treatment so you have to put a restriction on the number of areas of OCD to challenge at a time.

Grading the hierarchy

The ultimate goal of the hierarchy is to generate a list of feared situations and stimuli and related compulsions and order them from easiest to tackle (first rung of the ladder) to hardest (top of the ladder).

This task is best achieved with the client's personalised anxiety rating scale in front of them.

You can ask your client which of the situations or triggers identified in the brainstorm would be easiest to enter first. Once you have three or four compulsions or triggers, order them in list format. Do this visually on a whiteboard, or a sheet of paper. It may be helpful to use things that can be moved around so they can be changed, such as sticky notes, or type it on a computer.

Take each situation or trigger that has been identified and ask how anxious the client would feel if they could not do the compulsion or if they had to face the trigger without engaging in a ritual. It is important to keep anchoring using the client's anxiety rating scale. Place each trigger or situation on the visual 'ladder' or sheet so they can be seen. Then move on to the next step and ask the same, placing it above or below the previous one depending on their rating.

If the client is finding it hard to imagine how difficult certain tasks would be, consider generating the hierarchy in vivo. Once you have a few steps on the hierarchy, these can be used as reference points for further steps.

It is important to be aware that not all clients will report feeling anxious when considering how it would feel to face triggers of OCD without engaging in rituals. Some clients will describe disgust or it not feeling 'just right' or feeling incomplete. In those instances, you may wish to consider an alternative rating scale to capture the feeling the rating of difficulty may be based on. It may be helpful to use the suggested adaptations described earlier in relation to developing an anxiety rating scale.

Filling in the gaps

If the hierarchy is looking top or bottom heavy, spend some time filling in the gaps so that your client gets visual confirmation of the staged, progressive approach that you will be taking in ERP.

It is helpful for people to complete their hierarchy as a homework task but may not be possible as a self-generated task for autistic clients. Your client can elicit help from a family member to complete their hierarchy. It is important to explain to your client the aim is not to get everything down on the hierarchy at this stage, but the goal is to have the range and a place to start.

Remember, you will get more information as the client begins to engage in ERP tasks and things may move around or get added to the hierarchy. The hierarchy should be reviewed regularly during the ERP phase of treatment and updated. It is also important to bear in mind that things on the top of the hierarchy may need to be broken into mini-hierarchies when you are doing ERP. It may be helpful to explain this to the client if they are feeling overwhelmed by looking at some of the higher steps. It is also important you flag up that things can move around once you start ERP so this does not come as a surprise when it happens in sessions.

Some autistic clients may feel particularly anxious as a result of seeing their greatest fears set out 'on paper' and also worry that setting things out so explicitly will make the problem worse. If your client has a lot of avoidance behaviour this may well be the case. Be sensitive to this and emphasise that harder tasks will only be attempted after a lot of prior preparation. It is important for the client to know that they will never have to do something they do not want to do. While it is important not to make your client overly anxious by discussing potential exposure tasks, do not underestimate how therapeutic the process can be. For many, this is the first time they will have 'broken a challenge down' and considered that there are shades of grey to previously black and white fears.

Tanisha's hierarchy

Remember Tanisha with transformation obsessions of turning into her school bully and fears of transporting to another dimension? She has now completed psycho-education on anxiety and has created an anxiety rating scale where she has used her special interest in horses to understand different levels of anxiety and has managed to pair numbers 0 to 10 with these different levels. Tanisha understands what OCD is and has been able to articulate what she thinks is OCD and what is not. However, given that she is avoiding school at present, her insight into OCD is poor and she struggled to think of steps for her hierarchy. She was clear that her goal was to get back to education, but wanted to go to another school instead as she could not see a way of going back to the same school. Her mother and grandparents wanted her to return to her current school but also wanted her to have help with the rituals around the house where she would get stuck for up to an hour going back and forth over thresholds. Tanisha also found it frustrating getting stuck around her house so was keen to work on this, but less sure about working towards going back to the same school.

Tanisha agreed that her mother and grandparents could join the session on developing a hierarchy. They agreed to all write down concrete goals they wanted to work towards as OCD was getting them all involved. Tanisha said that she wanted to be able to walk around her house freely without getting stuck between rooms. Her mother wanted her to return to school and her grandparents wanted her to be able to access education by having schoolwork sent home, which would be avoiding behaviour. The goals were put on sticky notes and everyone was asked to write on a sticky note where they thought Tanisha was at now in relation to each goal and then think together about the steps she would need to take from where she was now to the goal. She was asked to rate each step in terms of how anxious she would feel if she had to take the step. She struggled to predict this, so the therapist arranged a home session to try out different scenarios to help her rate her anxiety. Below is an example of one goal hierarchy.

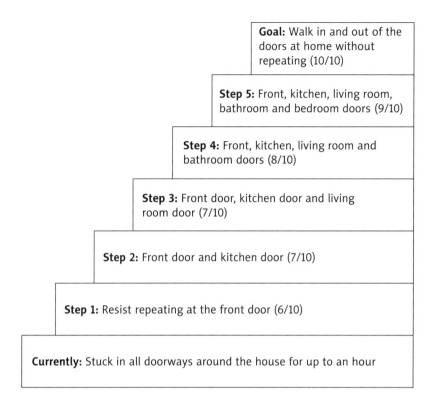

Goal: Walk in and out of the doors at home without repeating (10/10)

Step 5: Front, kitchen, living room, bathroom and bedroom doors (9/10)

Step 4: Front, kitchen, living room and bathroom doors (8/10)

Step 3: Front door, kitchen door and living room door (7/10)

Step 2: Front door and kitchen door (7/10)

Step 1: Resist repeating at the front door (6/10)

Currently: Stuck in all doorways around the house for up to an hour

Carrying out ERP tasks
Introduce ERP

It is important, particularly with your autistic client, to remind them of the rationale behind ERP and that the tools they have developed so far have been for this part of treatment – anxiety psycho-education, rating scale and hierarchy. You may find with your client that you will have to remind them throughout treatment of the rationale to help them link the principles behind the tasks to the concrete examples. This is how it was explained to Tanisha:

> T: *ERP is a very well-researched and effective approach for treating OCD. It involves putting ourselves in situations that we fear without doing any rituals or compulsions. By doing this, we can break the OCD cycle. We realise that we can cope and that the things we fear will happen don't turn out to be true.*

Chose a starting point

Assist your client to think of a potential starting point for the exposure process. You may find that you will need to be quite directive in supporting your client in choosing a task as they may struggle to make a decision. For the first task, it is best to choose a task that is likely to have a good chance of success, i.e. the client will face the trigger and resist engaging in the compulsion. This first step is an opportunity to learn how to go about doing exposure while providing the chance for an early confidence boost.

Plan the ERP task

When conducting tasks with autistic clients, it is important to operationalise the ERP task fully, i.e. be as explicit as possible about exactly what is involved. You should always write the task down (e.g., what object is to be touched, with what part of the body, for how long) and when the client will do the tasks. You will need to generate specific and clear recording sheets for any ERP, to be completed as homework. Discuss with your client beforehand exactly when they will do the tasks, where, and who else might help. Setting reminders on their phone to help them remember can be useful and help keep homework on track. Remember that impairments in executive function can be a feature of autism and this means organising, planning, generating and generalising are not key strengths for this client group.

While it can be helpful with non-autistic clients to alter or extend an exposure task once it has begun, with an autistic client try to keep ERP as predictable as possible. Generate a routine for this aspect of the treatment so it can have a degree of predictability and certainty about it, even though it is anxiety provoking. For example, be sure to specify exactly what the client is going to touch, with what part of the body, for how long, without doing exactly which specific compulsions.

Therapists may find it helpful to set rules for tasks to help them feel predictable; these can be the steps to completing tasks or an agreement of how the client will carry out tasks, for example once discussed it will be started within ten seconds.

Doing ERP tasks

Once the task has been detailed and set out, your role is to assist the client to expose themselves to the feared situation as fully as possible. Some clients may need to see the task modelled to them beforehand, so you or a family member could demonstrate the task. For autistic people, it may be helpful to be able to watch the task being done because of difficulties with imagination and future-thinking. Be aware that for some clients, the task being modelled may provide reassurance that nothing bad happens and so they may not feel anxious as you have been the person to test it out. Alternatively, modelling can be helpful not only to give a visual demonstration, but also to gather evidence that nothing bad happens. Modelling can also be used to demonstrate how something may typically be done, for example what a 'normal' handwash looks like.

Make sure you both know what 'baseline' anxiety means for your client. Our experience has been that autistic clients rarely describe themselves as 0 on an anxiety scale and tend to report a baseline level of 3/4 out of 10 on a typical anxiety scale. Taking an anxiety rating immediately before an ERP task may capture anticipatory anxiety, so you may wish to try to capture baseline at beginning of session, just before the task and then when the task has started.

Once the task has started, monitor anxiety using a rating scale every five minutes or at temporal intervals that seem appropriate. Throughout the ERP task, assist the client to monitor any changes in their anxiety or arousal levels. This is important modelling and part of the routine for ERP. Ask in the same way each time at the same intervals. Use the shared communication strategies or approaches developed during education about emotions, for example using the client's own language to describe their distress and a visual means of rating this distress. We would recommend that you plot the anxiety rated during ERP on a graph. Some clients will struggle to recognise subtle changes in their anxiety levels, in which case you could consider expanding the intervals when you ask for ratings from five minutes so they notice changes or use other techniques highlighted in the psycho-education phase of treatment.

During ERP, the therapist should assume a quite directive approach, taking on the role of an 'exposure coach' while also emphasising that it is the client's choice as to what tasks the client will complete (to increase their perception of responsibility for change and ownership of any subsequent success). Ensure that the client's attention remains focused on the ERP (e.g., *'Now pay close attention to what you have just done; notice that the contamination has been spread to all parts of your body'*).

Your client may be unsure of what constitutes 'normal' or non-OCD behaviour. This means that they will find it difficult to know what behaviour they should revert to once they have discontinued ERP. As well as therapists modelling 'normal' behaviour, you could do surveys and ask people how long they spend doing day-to-day tasks that your client's OCD has impacted on. This can give a useful guide as to what they could be working towards when engaged in ERP tasks; for example, what is a 'normal' handwash?

When is the task complete?

Clinical guidance suggests that ERP is successfully completed when the client's anxiety has habituated, and a 50 per cent reduction in the initial anxiety on starting the task is used as a general 'rule of thumb' (Steketee 1993). Some studies have found that autistic people have chronically high arousal levels which will impact on reports of 'baseline' anxiety levels and expectations around the fear extinction response (e.g., Top *et al.* 2016). Consequently, it is really important to get an accurate measure of your client's baseline anxiety before they begin the ERP task and together define what 'habituation' means on the anxiety scale. It may be that their baseline anxiety before the task is higher than the 50 per cent reduction anxiety point after they have completed the task, therefore it may be unrealistic to expect their anxiety to halve when it was high to begin with. For example, Tanisha's baseline anxiety before one of her tasks was 4 out of 10, but when she completed her ERP task it went up to 6 out of 10. Therefore, using the habituation rule of thumb was not an indicator of her habituating as her baseline anxiety was higher than the 50 per cent reduction mark (3 out of 10). In such instances, the goal would be for the client to get back to their baseline level of anxiety – for Tanisha this was 4 out of 10. In order for the client to experience habituation, you may wish to consider extending the session time if you notice their anxiety takes a while to habituate. If possible, you may leave a client to do the task and then check in later.

There are lots of issues that can interfere with successful ERP and these are not unique to autistic clients. Refer to a general OCD treatment text for the issues relevant to ERP with all clients (see the 'Books' section of Chapter 7). Issues can include reliance on the therapist for subtle reassurance giving during exposure, transferring responsibility for the feared consequence to the therapist as they 'told them to do it', using distraction and other anxiety-reducing activities to avoid complete exposure, storing up rituals to 'do later' and engaging in covert rituals during sessions. These are all indications that revisiting the rationale for ERP as a treatment model may be needed with your client.

Use of anxiety management techniques such as breathing exercises and employing distraction during ERP means that your client will not fully experience exposure and thus habituation of the anxiety. Thus, these are generally contra-indicated. However, some autistic people are very sensitive to becoming anxious and find it an intolerable experience. They will be reluctant to engage fully with ERP and probably have a marked tendency to avoid all anxiety-provoking situations. First, make sure your client does have procedural anxiety management strategies that are effective and helpful for use generally. Ideally, this is work that will have been undertaken at the early psycho-education stage.

If absolutely needed, you can work with your client to implement anxiety management prior to an ERP task so that they begin from a more relaxed state. We would suggest exploring other options to manage this first, such as breaking tasks down into smaller steps or implementing cognitive techniques to loosen some of the thinking around this. However, if all else fails, anxiety management techniques could be used as a stepping stone to help clients to approach the exposure task, but it is important this is put on the hierarchy with the view of starting exposure with anxiety management techniques and then dropping these once confidence has increased. This way, you are making it clear that the ultimate goal is still to engage in exposure without these techniques, but you are recognising they may be needed in the first instance.

In terms of distraction, it is important to look out for any subtle rituals or clients finding ways to bring their anxiety down, such as distraction. The most effective way to conduct ERP tasks is to do both in vivo and imaginal exposure (Abramowitz, Whiteside and Deacon 2005). This could be by asking clients to engage in a running dialogue to focus on the stimuli, which is a way of making sure they are fully engaged in the exposure without them getting distracted. However, if you have a very anxiety-sensitive client, who is reluctant to engage with the initial stages of ERP, you can make careful use of distraction. A distracting activity during ERP initially may encourage your client to engage with the ERP task but you must ensure that this becomes a step on the hierarchy, i.e. the first step of the ladder is being in the feared situation with a distracting activity and not doing the ritual; the second step of the ladder is being in the feared situation without the distracting activity (or partial use of) and not doing the ritual, and so on.

It is important to keep in mind that you are likely to find that ERP work with people with ASD will take longer than with other clients. They may prefer to take smaller steps up their hierarchy (as they may be overwhelmed with anxiety), may need more repetitions to achieve mastery and can find it harder to generalise their success from one area to another. It may also take longer for their anxiety to dissipate. You may wish to add extra sessions to accommodate the slower pace of work.

ERP as homework

Repeating and extending the ERP tasks between sessions (homework) is a very important part of treatment. As a minimum, aim for multiple repetitions of the in-session completed task if this was successful.

By now you should be familiar as a therapist with the need to be clear, explicit, structured and directive. Plan and schedule the homework tasks with your client.

One useful idea is to put together a timetable of the week and then schedule in ERP practice. This means it can become part of the daily/weekly routine. Clearly detail when the client will practise, where they will be and if they need anyone to prompt or help them, and detail the steps needed to complete the tasks.

Your client may benefit from having visuals in the areas at home that may trigger rituals to remind them to resist the compulsion; for example, Tanisha had signs on doors to remind her not to walk in and out of them.

Give your client a means of recording the homework tasks and the anxiety ratings in the same way they did in the sessions so that this can be reviewed. This can be done on paper handouts, on a mobile phone or tablet or any other way they may find accessible.

It is really important for clients to have support in place to do tasks both in and out of sessions. Try and identify a co-therapist such as a family member and train them up to support your client with homework. Make sure the client and family have shared, clear guidelines on tasks to reduce the chance of disagreement when the client is engaged in ERP, and that your client is consenting to this approach.

If your client is really struggling to engage with ERP, you could think together about whether there is anyone else who is usually involved in completing rituals or compulsions (often a family member). Perhaps they can be the first step in changing the ritual. Again, this would become the first step on the hierarchy and should be written and recorded as such. Your client, the family member and you as therapist can plan how the third party can change their response in the OCD situation. This could give your client the chance to experience their anxiety habituating when challenging OCD, but without having to resist a compulsion.

Going back to Tanisha, she struggled to start doing ERP tasks as she did not want to work on things related to her returning to school as they felt too high on her hierarchy. She attempted tasks in relation to resisting stepping back and forth over thresholds and tried to do this with the front door first. However, she struggled to resist the ritual even with encouragement and support from her family. Three ERP sessions had taken place where everyone thought about options for the task but Tanisha explained she just found it too hard as it felt automatic to do it. The therapist discussed other options where someone else could try and stand up to OCD for her and they explored options in the sessions. The therapist suggested that her family did not give reassurance when she asked an OCD question. Tanisha found this hard to think about, so they agreed they would just start with one type of OCD question that she asked which was, *'Am I still on planet earth?'* The family agreed they would all answer consistently and say, *'I am not answering the OCD question.'* Tanisha predicted her anxiety would be 6/10, which she found scary, but agreed it would be easier for others to stand up to OCD. They practised in the session and every day for homework, and Tanisha found it did get easier to tolerate not having the answer.

What to do if a client cannot do ERP tasks?

Many clients struggle to resist engaging in compulsions following exposure and they can often happen rapidly or covertly or be quickly substituted with other forms of neutralisation. As we have emphasised, the ideal outcome is for the client to completely stop or inhibit all compulsive or ritualistic behaviours from the first exposure trial onwards. However, if this feels too difficult, the client can be encouraged to gradually alter or reduce rituals or compulsions. This can include breaking the task down further, delaying rituals and then extending the time, cutting down the rituals, messing them up or substituting rituals with another behaviour. These can be useful steps to build up your client's sense of having some control over the compulsions.

Ritual replacement, rewards and routines

A pattern of restricted, repetitive behaviour, routines and activities is a core characteristic of autism. OCD can take up a lot of time. Successful treatment can leave empty time in a schedule. Furthermore, autistic people can lack the opportunities to access meaningful and pleasurable activities and occupations. As a therapist, you need to be sensitive to what might take the place of OCD in a person's life. When progress is being made and OCD rituals are reducing, discuss with your client what they might do in the newly freed-up spaces in their schedule. Think about new routines and activities that can take the place of OCD. Discuss with your client what will be rewarding and pleasurable for them. Don't be afraid to discuss concrete rewards as well as rewarding activities. Your client may have been working hard, but in the absence of a job or busy social life, getting better from OCD might not be inherently rewarding itself. Harold was motivated to change his OCD because he had a college place and he wanted to be able to function well at college. If he had not had a college place and a motivating course to attend, he might have been vulnerable to rapid relapse of any OCD treatment gains, because there were no external factors rewarding him for getting better, or 'nothing to work for'. This is why learning about your client's daily life, routines and schedule at the outset offers valuable information in planning treatment.

Generalising: spreading and sharing the gains

You may notice your client manages ERP tasks in some areas and then struggles to generalise learning from tasks in other areas. For example, they can do a task in the session but then struggle to apply it to other settings outside the sessions or they can follow ERP principles for one set of symptoms but they cannot readily apply them to other areas of their OCD. This difficulty around generalising can make progress very slow and you may be concerned about whether your client will use tools they have gained beyond therapy.

There is no easy solution to this difficulty, but there are things you can weave into ERP work so that you are encouraging clients to generalise. It is good to try and do the following throughout this phase of treatment:

- *Golden ERP rules:* It may be useful to write three or four key steps to setting up ERP tasks and then use the same set of rules for any task to demonstrate that the same rules apply regardless of the task.

- *Discuss similarities between tasks:* It is helpful to explicitly discuss what is similar between the tasks and maybe make a list of all similar triggers or tasks to highlight this.

- *List what they can now do after the task:* Similar to the above suggestion, after the task you should spend time exploring what has been learned about the area of concern and then say, *'Now you have been able to do this task, this means you should be able to do...'*, to highlight concrete examples of what the client possibly can now do.

- *Use of family:* As mentioned above, involving a co-therapist to reiterate messages from sessions and point out similarities between tasks can be helpful to support the client.

- *Fading support:* It is useful to try and do this as soon as possible to give the client the opportunity to trial the techniques themselves so you can see where they may need more support.

Going back to Tanisha, the therapist spent time working on this with her throughout her treatment. Tanisha struggled throughout treatment to see that when she had managed to overcome repeating waking over thresholds at her bedroom door, this was the same as the bathroom and kitchen door in her home. Her therapist spoke about the similarities between the doors and came up with these rules:

I know its OCD when I:

- *get a horrible thought*

- *feel scared*

- *want to keep stepping back and forth.*

All the doorways are the same.

When I feel like this, resist OCD. It will feel hard at first but gets easier.

Ask Mum to help if I get stuck.

Getting cognitive if you need to

While traditional ERP approaches focus on assisting the client to experience anxiety extinction following repeated exposure to feared stimuli, cognitive behavioural approaches to ERP include an element of cognitive reappraisal.

In treatment as usual, the obsession and feared outcome are clearly identified in preparation for the task. Part of the routine of ERP is post-hoc to examine whether the feared consequence did or did not occur. It is important clients get learning not just about anxiety habituating but also in relation to their OCD fears. This is not always possible to test directly, especially when the fears may be untestable, for example fear of going to hell, or getting a life-threatening condition in the future.

We have found that autistic clients with OCD are no different from other populations with OCD in having specific OCD beliefs and worries about what will happen if they don't perform compulsions.

In treatment as usual, it can be helpful to use cognitive techniques to rebalance appraisals and beliefs. This often means emphasising aspects of the client's experience during ERP that do not fit with their OCD beliefs and appraisals and accumulating data that supports an alternative way of thinking. For example, Harold has strong beliefs that he will get ill if he comes into contact with others' saliva. A cognitive approach might include researching how germs are transmitted, the likelihood of transmission by saliva, and reviewing this information with Harold. Rigid, inflexible thinking can be a feature of autism and amending beliefs to incorporate 'grey' information can be difficult. Thus, adapted CBT for autism has a behavioural emphasis.

However, there are some occasions when it seems that cognitive change techniques might be needed to try and loosen appraisals or beliefs so that a client can engage with ERP (see Wilhelm and Steketee 2006 for a useful guide).

Therapist tips

- Develop a predictable and structured routine for ERP; ensure your client is clear about exactly what they (and others) will do and that this is written down.

- Model the task(s) if needed.

- Clarify what a return to 'baseline' of anxiety might look like.

- Anticipate longer duration of ERP tasks as anxiety can take time to dissipate.

- Plan and write down homework tasks so they are specific, concrete and scheduled.

- Suggest the use of a phone alarm or app to help remind client of the homework schedule.

- Design recording sheets for your client to monitor progress between sessions.

- Consider scheduling 'replacement' activities as OCD behaviours reduce.

- Remember that incentives can be helpful when encouraging people to introduce new events and situations into their daily repertoire.

- Note that we have not found 'loop tapes' providing endless exposure to obsessional thoughts helpful with this client group. The treatment rationale is not readily accessible, quite abstract and can be confusing.

Chapter 6

CBT PHASE 3 RELAPSE PREVENTION

Agenda

- Introducing the relapse prevention phase
- Identify possible triggers
- Identify warning signs of relapse
- Develop an action plan
- Manage residual symptoms
- Follow-up sessions
- Therapist tips

Introducing the relapse prevention phase

In OCD, a response to treatment is indicated by a reduction of 35 per cent or more on a measure such as the CY-BOCS (Goodman *et al.* 1991). Remission is considered if diagnostic criteria for OCD are no longer met, or if a CY-BOCS score of less than 12 is seen, for at least a week. Recovery is indicated by remission criteria being present for 12 months. A relapse is indicated by the client no longer meeting criteria of treatment response, remission or recovery for a least a month (Mataix-Cols *et al.* 2016).

The relapse prevention phase of treatment typically takes place over the last two sessions of treatment. It is a core component of CBT for OCD with evidence suggesting that including it in treatment leads to better long-term outcomes (Hiss, Foa and Kozak 1994). There is very limited research into this component of treatment in general and no studies on the impact of including relapse prevention in treatment of OCD in those with autism. However, from clinical experience this is seen as an essential part of treatment, particularly for those with autism for whom it is helpful to have a concrete plan along with ideas on how to generalise what they have learned in sessions to other situations.

When completing this phase of treatment, it is important to embed this within the wider treatment programme, including any successful adaptations. If an autistic person with OCD has responded or remitted, then this phase of treatment can be completed as set out. However, if there has not been a successful treatment response, then you will need to consider whether you should continue with ERP sessions if you feel further gains may be made. This is not unusual for autistic clients who may require a longer course of treatment. If you plan to end treatment and your client has not demonstrated a 'treatment response', then the last portion of the sessions may not be about relapse prevention but rather thinking about identifying barriers to treatment and possible ways of overcoming these. This may include consideration of other treatment options as outlined in the clinical guidelines (NICE 2005). In both scenarios, it is helpful to review treatment and discuss what the person has learned and the tools they have gained to fight OCD.

It is good to start the session by reviewing the goals set in phase one of treatment and assessing progress towards these. It is also good for clients to write a list of the gains made in treatment as well as the key learning points taken from the sessions. It is important that autistic clients write this in their own words. As in other phases of treatment, your client may benefit from using visual cues, photographs and so on.

Introducing the concept of relapse prevention is particularly important for autistic clients who may not anticipate future changes in symptoms and may find this particularly distressing if it does occur. A good way of introducing relapse prevention is to use the concept of setting out a plan to manage setbacks and blips following the end of treatment. It is important to explain to clients that setbacks are likely to happen, and it is particularly important to normalise this given common problems managing change. It is also important to emphasise that a setback or a lapse does not indicate a relapse, and that these relapse prevention sessions are to help plan for setbacks so they do not lead to a relapse. The conversation in introducing relapse prevention could start like this:

> T: *We are now going to think about the future and how to manage when OCD symptoms try to come back. It is important for you to know this is completely normal and we expect this to happen, especially in the first year after treatment ends. We are going to spend the next two sessions putting together a plan of action. This will include thinking about times when OCD is most likely to try and come back, what the warning signs might be and then what to do about it.*

Identify possible triggers

First, explain to the client that it is often at times of stress that OCD comes back. Spend some time listing possible stressors that the client may face in the foreseeable future. It is useful to think about any potential stressors that are coming up between now and the next follow-up session, so that the client can break things down into smaller periods of time that are not too open-ended (see follow-up sessions section below for more detail). Possible triggers can be broken down into two categories: general triggers and specific OCD triggers.

In terms of general life stressors, these are largely the same as they are for individuals without OCD. Additional common stressors for autistic clients may be times of change or transition (such as leaving college or moving home). Ending OCD treatment may be a potential stressor in that it is a change from a routine and the loss of social contact with the therapist. OCD-specific triggers are those that would involve a client facing their fears. For instance, in the case of Harold it was going on an all-inclusive holiday with his family where all the food was included. Despite Harold working hard in treatment and having overcome his fears, this was recognised as a potential trigger given that he had to face this fear for over a week.

Be as concrete and specific as possible when identifying potential stressors. This may include drawing a timeline of when stressors are likely to happen. This will reduce the likelihood of the client feeling caught off guard. The aim is to make things as predictable as possible. As part of treatment, it is important to think about stressors in general and about whether there are measures that can be put in place that could help reduce stress overall. For example, attending social skills training or working on social anxiety may help an autistic person to reduce additional stress of being in social situations. This is important in that it builds strengths in clients and a range of positive activities for them to engage in.

Identify warning signs of relapse

The task in this part of the relapse prevention plan is to support the client to identify the potential warning signs of OCD returning. Here are some potential questions the therapist can ask:

What would it look or feel like if you knew OCD was coming back?

What do you remember about what it was like when it started? Is that how it would feel and look like?

What obsessions and compulsions do you think would come back first? This could be the thing we last worked on, the one you found hardest to get rid of or the one that you had the longest.

What do you think you would not be able to do which may give us a sign OCD is coming back, for example eat out at restaurants?

Research evidence has found that when people relapse and new symptoms develop, they are most likely to be in the same symptom dimension as was experienced previously, such as contamination, harm and so on (Fernández de la Cruz *et al.* 2013). It is helpful to get family members, partners or another person involved at this point, if the client consents, and ask them what they think they would see if OCD was coming back. This is particularly important as some autistic clients may struggle to identify these signs for themselves. It is important to agree a plan as to how they will let the client know they have noticed this; for example, should they say it as soon as they have noticed? What language should they use to talk about the OCD?

As well as considering warning signs, autistic clients may benefit from an explanation of when not to worry, in particular in relation to intrusive thoughts. You may have discussed this earlier in treatment but it is important to recap any psycho-education work on intrusive thoughts. The key message is that the client should expect to experience thoughts they do not like, and that the key is not to respond to them by engaging in a ritual. Sharing a survey such as the one published by Purdon and Clark (1993) can be a helpful way to normalise intrusive thoughts. You could introduce some mindfulness techniques in the relapse prevention phase of treatment such as 'letting go' of thoughts. The hope is at this stage of treatment that the power of the intrusive thoughts will have reduced and so clients are more able to implement such techniques.

It is important to highlight to the client that once they have noticed warning signs it is best to act early by implementing their action plan.

Develop an action plan

An individualised action plan will increase the chance of it being helpful. In this part of the plan, the goal is to support your client to detail how they will use tools from CBT to push back OCD, i.e. ERP.

A useful thing to do is list the 'golden rules' for fighting OCD. The golden rules can be applied to any symptom that (re)emerges. They could include:

- Identify OCD symptoms.

- Make a hierarchy.

- Set up an ERP task.

- Remember that anxiety comes down the more you do the task.

- Do the task every day.

It might be helpful for your client to have photos of how they have completed ERP tasks before, or the steps to engaging in ERP tasks. This may be a helpful reminder of the golden rules but also evidence that they have done it before and they can do it again.

As part of the action plan it is helpful to discuss with the client and their family what they can do to help and to write that on the action plan. Commonly, the client may want help from a friend, relative or carer in identifying symptoms or carrying out ERP tasks. Another thing to consider is if rituals have in the past involved family members, they need to be clear on what to do if the client starts to ask for this to happen again in future. For example, what do they need to do if the client starts to ask for reassurance or asks for a routine to change to accommodate OCD? In cases where family accommodation has been significant in the past, it may be helpful for family members to have their own action plan. For example, if they have been asked for reassurance, share with client that it is OCD making them ask and then agree a plan of how they are going to respond. It is important that the client knows what to expect and that it is a predictable, as well as collaborative, plan.

Manage residual symptoms

If there are residual symptoms at the end of treatment this increases the risk of relapse. It is important to share this with the client and explain the importance of challenging all symptoms of OCD. The following analogy could be useful and you could consider drawing it out as you explain:

> T: *I want to explain the importance of overcoming all of your symptoms of OCD by using an analogy. I want you to picture a weed; you want to get rid of the weed so you try by cutting the leaves off. Do you think that will get rid of the weed?*
>
> C: *No, it will just keep growing back.*
>
> T: *That's correct! What do you think the best way is to get rid of the weed?*
>
> C: *You could use weed killer?*
>
> T: *That's a good idea. Another way is to pull the weed out from the root to make sure there is no chance of it growing back. That's what you have to do with OCD; you have to get rid of it completely so that there is less chance of it coming back.*

If your client can use this analogy, this can be helpful to draw on in the final two sessions to target any residual symptoms of OCD. You may also be able to use it to plan homework tasks in the period before any follow-up sessions. You may wish to consider over-learning tasks that were described in the previous section.

Follow-up sessions

It is advisable, if your service permits, to arrange follow-up sessions over a period of 12 months. Evidence suggests relapse is more likely to happen in the 12 months following CBT for OCD (Barrett *et al.* 2005). We recommend offering follow-up sessions at one, three, six and 12 months following the end of treatment, with graded increase in gaps between sessions. These sessions are particularly important for clients with ASD who may need more support to generalise this learning from treatment and who may struggle to apply principles to any new symptoms that may arise. You may find that as well as reviewing progress and the relapse prevention plan in these sessions, clients with ASD benefit from conducting ERP tasks.

If your client experiences a relapse, it is advisable to offer some booster sessions to help them to overcome this. Treatment guidelines recommend that if a relapse occurs within 12 months of completing treatment, clients should be offered further CBT sessions with minimal wait – they should go to the top of treatment waiting lists (NICE 2005). You may find autistic clients may benefit from booster sessions at times when they are struggling to implement their relapse prevention plan or manage new symptoms.

If booster sessions are offered, it is important to think through with your client what may need to be different with the second round of treatment. There may be variables that may have impacted on treatment success, such as not completing tasks or not enough involvement from significant others. It may be that some symptoms were not disclosed or they never confronted a core fear. It is important to be clear and explicit about what you think may have led to relapse and what you think will help. You can develop a collaborative treatment contract with your client; this is particularly helpful for autistic people as it is then clear what the expectations are for further treatment.

Therapist tips

- Encourage clients to try to continue the routine of having check-ins on their OCD and thinking about how to tackle it. Autistic clients may like this idea as it keeps a routine of sessions going.

- Develop a written relapse prevention plan, including visual reminders and cues.

- Suggest having the relapse prevention plan displayed somewhere where the client will see it regularly. You can make several copies to put around in places and maybe in areas of hotspots for OCD.

- Offer follow-up sessions at graded intervals – fade out treatment.

Final words

We hope this workbook is helpful. We find this clinical work enjoyable and creative and we learn about lots of interesting things as well as autism and OCD.

WORKSHEET: TANISHA'S RELAPSE PREVENTION PLAN

Triggers	What are potential stressful things coming up?

General, e.g. exams, change in routine, etc.

- ☐ Change in my routine at home – getting up early every day for school
- ☐ Mum going back to work

OCD related, e.g. holiday

- ☐ Going back into classes at school
- ☐ Seeing my school bully

Warning signs	How would you know OCD is coming back?

What would it look or feel like, e.g. handwashing more, avoiding eating at restaurants?

- ☐ Get lots of horrible thoughts and get scared
- ☐ Ask Mum, Nan and Grandad OCD questions

Which symptoms are most likely to return?

- ☐ OCD questions
- ☐ Getting stuck in doorways

What else would you or other people notice, e.g. asking for reassurance, being more upset with others?

- ☐ Ask my family lots of OCD questions

Action plan	What should you do?

Remember – ACT EARLY!

What are the golden rules for fighting OCD?

- ☐ Remember anxiety always comes down and OCD tricks me
- ☐ Trigger OCD on purpose and practise not listening
- ☐ Use my hierarchy to help it feel less hard

Remember – DO ERP!

What can others do to help?

- ☐ Have an OCD meeting with Mum, Nan and Grandad to talk about any tasks I need to do
- ☐ Family to tell me at meeting if they have seen OCD around
- ☐ Do my tasks with me

WORKSHEET: TEMPLATE FOR RELAPSE PREVENTION PLAN

Triggers	What are potential stressful things coming up?

General, e.g. exams, change in routine etc.

☐ _____

☐ _____

OCD related, e.g. holiday

☐ _____

☐ _____

Warning signs	How would you know OCD is coming back?

What would it look or feel like, e.g. handwashing more, avoiding eating at restaurants?

☐ _____

☐ _____

Which symptoms are most likely to return?

☐ _____

☐ _____

What else would you or other people notice, e.g. asking for reassurance, being more upset with others?

☐ _____

☐ _____

Action plan	What should you do?

Remember – ACT EARLY!

What are the golden rules for fighting OCD?

- ☐ _____
- ☐ _____
- ☐ _____

Remember – DO ERP!

What can others do to help?

- ☐ _____
- ☐ _____
- ☐ _____

Chapter 7

RESOURCES AND REFERENCES

The handouts cam be downloaded at www.jkp.com/voucher using the code KYEWAZO.

Websites

OCD charities:

- www.ocdaction.org.uk

- www.ocduk.org

Autism charity:

- www.autism.org.uk

Social stories resources:

- www.autism.org.uk/about/strategies/social-stories-comic-strips.aspx

Publications

Attwood, T. (2004) *Exploring Feelings: Cognitive Behaviour Therapy to Manage Anxiety*. Arlington, TX: Future Horizons.

Attwood, T. (2008) *The Complete Guide to Asperger's Syndrome*. London: Jessica Kingsley Publishers.

Gaus, V.L. (2007) *Cognitive-Behavioral Therapy for Adult Asperger Syndrome*. New York, NY: Guilford Press.

Gaus, V.L. (2011) *Living Well on the Spectrum: How to Use your Strengths to Meet the Challenges of Asperger Syndrome/High-Functioning Autism.* New York, NY: Guilford Press.

Gray, C. (2015) *The New Social Story™ Book* (revised and expanded 15th anniversary edition). Arlington, TX: Future Horizons.

March, J.S. and Mulle, K. (1998) *OCD in Children and Adolescents: A Cognitive-Behavioral Treatment Manual.* New York, NY: Guilford Press.

Menzies, R.G. and de Silva, P. (eds) (2003) *Obsessive-Compulsive Disorder Theory, Research and Treatment.* Chichester: John Wiley & Sons.

Shafran, R., Frampton, I., Heyman, I., Reynolds, M., Teachman, B., Rachman, S. (2003) 'The preliminary development of a new self-report measure for OCD in young people.' *Journal of Adolescence* 26, 137–142.

Stallard, P. (2002) *Think Good, Feel Good: A Cognitive Behaviour Therapy Workbook for Children and Young People.* New York, NY: Wiley. (The worksheet about the fight or flight response has clear explanations with visual cues to aid concepts. We have found it is acceptable to adults although intended primarily for use with young people.)

References

Abramowitz, J., Whiteside, S.P. and Deacon, B.J. (2005) 'The effectiveness of treatment for pediatric obsessive-compulsive disorder: a meta-analysis.' *Behavior Therapy* 36(1), 55–63.

American Psychiatric Association (2013) *Diagnostic and Statistical Manual of Mental Disorders* (fifth edition). Washington, DC.

Anderson, S. and Morris, J. (2006) 'Cognitive behaviour therapy for people with Asperger syndrome.' *Behavioural and Cognitive Psychotherapy* 34(3), 293–303.

Angold, A. and Costello, E.J. (1987) Mood and Feelings Questionnaire (MFQ). Durham, NC: Developmental Epidemiology Program, Duke University.

Barrett, P., Farrell, L., Dadds, M. and Boulter, N. (2005) 'Cognitive-behavioural family treatment of childhood obsessive-compulsive disorder: long term follow-up and predictors of treatment outcome.' *Journal of the American Academy of Child and Adolescent Psychiatry* 44(10), 1005–1014.

Beck, A.T., Steer, R.A. and Brown, G.K. (1996) *BDI-II: Beck Depression Inventory*. San Antonio, TX: Psychological Corporation.

Cadman, T., Spain, D., Johnston, P., Russell, A.J. *et al.* (2015) 'Obsessive-compulsive disorder in adults with high-functioning autism spectrum disorder: what does self-report with the OCI-R tell us?' *Autism Research* 8(5), 477–485.

Calvocoressi, L., Mazure, C.M., Kasl, S.V., Skolnick, J. *et al.* (1999) 'Family accommodation of obsessive-compulsive symptoms: instrument development and assessment of family behavior.' *The Journal of Nervous and Mental Disease* 187(10), 636–642.

Chorpita, B.F., Yim, L., Moffitt, C., Umemoto, L.A. and Francis, S.E. (2000) 'Assessment of symptoms of DSM-IV anxiety and depression in children: a revised child anxiety and depression scale.' *Behaviour Research and Therapy* 38(8), 835–855.

Chowdury, M., Benson, B.A. and Hillier, A. (2010) 'Changes in restricted repetitive behaviours with age: a study of high-functioning adults with autism spectrum disorders.' *Research in Autism Spectrum Disorders* 4, 210–216.

Connor, K.M., Davidson, J.R., Churchill, L.E., Sherwood, A., Weisler, R.H. and Foa, E. (2000) 'Psychometric properties of the Social Phobia Inventory (SPIN): new self-rating scale.' *The British Journal of Psychiatry* 176(4), 379–386.

Fernández de la Cruz, L., Micali, N., Roberts, S., Turner, C., Nakatani, E., Heyman, I. and Mataix-Cols, D. (2013) 'Are the symptoms of obsessive-compulsive disorder temporally stable in children/adolescents? A prospective naturalistic study.' *Psychiatry Research Neuroimaging* 209(2), 196–201.

Geller, D., Biederman, J., Jones, J., Park, K., Schwartz, S., Shapiro, S. and Coffey, B. (1998) 'Is juvenile obsessive-compulsive disorder a developmental subtype of the disorder? A review of the pediatric literature.' *Journal of the American Academy of Child and Adolescent Psychiatry* 37, 420–427

Goodman, W.K., Price, L.H., Rasmussen, S.A., Mazure, C. *et al.* (1989) 'Yale-Brown Obsessive Compulsive Scale (Y-BOCS).' *Archives of General Psychiatry* 46, 1006–1011.

Goodman, W.K., Price, L.H., Rasmussen, S.A., Riddle, M.A. and Rapoport, J.L. (1991) Children's Yale-Brown Obsessive Compulsive Scale (CY-BOCS). New Haven, CT: Department of Psychiatry, Yale University School of Medicine.

Hiss, H., Foa, E.B. and Kozak, M.J. (1994) 'Relapse prevention program for treatment of obsessive compulsive disorder.' *Journal of Consulting and Clinical Psychology* 62(4), 801–808.

Kenny, L, Hattersely, C., Molins, B., Buckley, C, Povey, C. and Pellicano, E. (2016) 'Which terms should be used to describe autism? Perspectives from the UK autism community.' *Autism* 20(4), 442–462.

Kroenke, K., Spitzer, R.L. and Williams, J.B. (2001) 'The PHQ-9.' *Journal of General Internal Medicine* 16(9), 606–613.

Kyrios, M. (2003) 'Exposure and Response Prevention for Obsessive-Compulsive Disorder.' In R.G. Menzies and P. de Silva (eds) *Obsessive Compulsive Disorder: Theory, Research and Treatment.* Chichester: John Wiley & Sons.

Leekham, S.R, Prior, M.R. and Uljarevic, M. (2011) 'Restricted and repetitive behaviours in autism spectrum disorders: a review of research in the last decade.' *Psychological Bulletin* 137(4), 562–593.

Liebowitz, M.R. (1987) 'Social phobia.' In D.F. Klein (ed.) *Anxiety.* Basel: Karger Publishers.

Lord, C, Rutter, M. and Le Couteur, A. (1994) 'Autism Diagnostic Interview-Revised: a revised version of a diagnostic interview for caregivers of individuals with possible pervasive developmental disorders.' *Journal of Autism and Developmental Disorders* 24, 659–685.

March, J.S. and Mulle, K. (1998) *OCD in Children and Adolescents: A Cognitive-Behavioral Treatment Manual.* New York, NY: Guilford Press.

Mataix-Cols, D.M., Fernández de la Cruz, L., Nordsletten, A., Lenhard, F., Isomura, K. and Simpson, H.B. (2016) 'Towards an international expert consensus for defining treatment response, recovery and relapse in obsessive compulsive disorder.' *World Psychiatry* 15(1), 80–81.

National Institute for Health and Care Excellence (2005) *Clinical Guidelines 31 Obsessive Compulsive Disorder and Body Dysmorphic Disorder: Treatment.* London: NICE.

National Institute for Health and Care Excellence (2012) *Clinical Guidelines 142 Autism Spectrum Disorder in Adults: Diagnosis and Management.* London: NICE.

Purdon, C. and Clark, D.A. (1993) 'Obsessive intrusive thoughts in non-clinical subjects. Part 1. Content and relation with depressive, anxious and obsessional symptoms.' *Behaviour Research and Therapy* 31, 713–720.

Russell, A.J., Jassi, A., Fullana, M.A., Mack, H. *et al.* (2013) 'Cognitive behaviour therapy for co-morbid obsessive compulsive disorder in high-functioning autism spectrum disorders: a randomized controlled trial.' *Depression and Anxiety* 30, 697–708.

Simpson, H.B., Marcus, S.M., Zuckoff, A., Franklin, M. and Foa, E.B. (2012) 'Patient adherence to cognitive-behavioral therapy predicts long-term outcome in obsessive-compulsive disorder.' *The Journal of Clinical Psychiatry* 73(9), 1265.

Spence, S.H. (1998) 'A measure of anxiety symptoms among children.' *Behaviour Research and Therapy.* 36(5), 545–566.

Steketee, G.S. (1993) *Treatment of Obsessive Compulsive Disorder.* New York, NY: Guilford Press.

Top, N., Stephenson, K., Doxey, C.R., Crowley, M., Brock-Kirwan, C. and South, M. (2016) 'Atypical amygdala response to fear conditioning in autism spectrum disorder.' *Biological Psychiatry* 1, 308–315.

Turner, M. (1999) 'Annotation: repetitive behaviour in autism: a review of psychological research.' *The Journal of Child Psychology and Psychiatry and Allied Disciplines* 40(6), 839–849.

Uher, R., Heyman, I., Turner, C.M. and Shafran, R. (2008) 'Self-, parent-report and interview measures of obsessive-compulsive disorder in children and adolescents.' *Journal of Anxiety Disorders* 22(6), 979–990.

Wilhelm, S. and Steketee, G.S. (2006) *Cognitive Therapy Obsessive Compulsive Disorder: A Guide for Professionals.* Oakland, CA: New Harbinger Publications.

INDEX

Abramowitz, J. 108
activities/interests 13–14
alexithymia, tips 26
American Psychiatric Association 15
Anderson, S. 23
Angold, A. 43
anxiety
  baselines 105, 106–7
  body maps 75–6
  exposure and response prevention
    (ERP) 84–92
  'fight or flight' response 71–2
  habituation 106–7
  intensity variation 74–5
  introducing ERP to client 91–2
  introducing rating 74, 76
  key considerations 70
  management/relaxation 79–83,
    107–8
  not doing compulsions 87–8
  physical aspects 70–1
  practicing use of rating scales 78–9
  rating 72–9
  rating during ERP 105–6
  rating scale options 76–8
  reduction over time 88–90
  repeated exposure 90–1
  social 64
  terminology 73
  treatment rationale 69–70
  understanding 70–2
  see also cognitive behaviour therapy
    (CBT)
assessment *see* OCD assessment

Autism Diagnostic Interview-Revised
  (ADI-R) 37
autism spectrum disorder (ASD)
  overview 13–14
  terminology 15–16
avoidance behaviours 63

Barrett, P. 123
Beck, A.T. 43
Beck Depression Inventory 43
behaviour change, goal of CBT 28
Benson, B.A. 39
body maps 42, 46–7
  anxiety 75–6
  'fight or flight' response 71–2
book, aims and approach 9–11
Brown, G.K. 43

Cadman, T. 42
Calvocoressi, L. 43
CBT-specific adaptations 27–9
central coherence 14
Children's Obsessive-Compulsive
  Inventory-Revised (ChOCI-R)
  42–3
Children's Yale-Brown Obsessive
  Compulsive Scale (CY-BOCS) 35
Chorpita, B.F. 43
Chowdury, M. 39
Clark, D.A. 121
cognitive behaviour therapy (CBT)
  booster sessions 124
  building blocks 92

cognitive behaviour therapy (CBT) *cont.*
  goal 28
  goal setting 53–6
  goal setting handout 55–6
  key considerations 50–1
  OCD psycho-education 57–62
  'thoughts-feelings-behaviour'
    framework 27–9
  treatment overview 49–52
  treatment overview handout 52
  treatment structure 50
  see also anxiety; exposure and
    response prevention (ERP);
    obsessive compulsive disorder
    (OCD); relapse prevention
cognitive components, OCD 65–6
cognitive reappraisal 113–14
collaborative working, with clients
  53, 63
communication 13
  adaptation 20–2
  non-verbal 21–2
  preferences 16
  tips 25
compulsions 35
  defining 61
  effects of not doing 87–8
Connor, K.M., 43
Costello, E.J. 43

daily living 64–5
Deacon, B.J. 108
*Diagnostic and Statistical Manual
  of Mental Disorders, version 5*
  (DSM-5) 15
disorder, defining 58
distraction 108

emotion recognition 14
emotional literacy 49–50
engagement 22
executive function 14, 27, 64–5
  tips 26
exposure and response prevention
  (ERP) 27, 49
  anxiety management 107–8
  anxiety rating 105–7

beginning treatment 84–5
carrying out tasks 103–11
client unable to do tasks 110–11
cognitive reappraisal 113–14
distraction 108
doing tasks 105–6
exposure coaching 106
generalisation 112–14
goals 107
golden rules 112–13
habituation 106–7
hierarchy creation *see* exposure
  hierarchy
as homework 109–10
introducing concept 103
introducing to client 91–2
key considerations 93
not doing compulsions 87–8
possible issues/problems 107
repeated exposure 90–1
rewards 111
ritual replacement 111
routines 104–5
rules for tasks 104–5
starting point 104
task completion 106–8
task modelling 105
task planning 104–5
timeframes 108–9
tips 114–15
treatment rationale 84
see also anxiety; cognitive behaviour
  therapy (CBT)
exposure hierarchy 94–103
  as cause of anxiety 101
  family/carer involvement 99
  filling in gaps 101
  framework 97
  generating ideas 98–9
  grading 100
  introducing concept 94–6
  purpose 94
  relating to OCD 96–7
  reviewing/amending 101
  Tanisha 102–3
eye contact 21

Family Accommodation Scale 43, 99
fear 71

feelings, in CBT 27–8
Fernández de la Cruz, L. 121
'fight or flight' response 71–2
follow-up sessions 123–4
formulation
    Harold 67
    OCD treatment 63–6

Geller, D. 39
generalisation, ERP 112–14
goal setting, CBT 53–6
Goodman, W.K. 35, 36

habituation 106–7
handouts
    CBT treatment overview 52
    goal setting 55–6
    OCD definitions worksheet 61
    OCD trap 62
    What is OCD? worksheet 60
Harold 111, 114, 120
    anxiety management 79–83
    exposure and response prevention
        (ERP) 84–7
    exposure hierarchy 94–7
    OCD formulation 67
Hillier, A. 39

images
    exposure hierarchy 94–6
    use of 10–11, 24, 58–9, 84–5
in vivo working 24
intellectual ability, and practical living
        skills 14

Kenny, L. 15
key considerations
    anxiety 70
    cognitive behaviour therapy (CBT)
        50–1
    exposure and response prevention
        (ERP) 93–4
Kroenke, K. 43
Kyrios, M. 10

language, use of 21, 121
Le Couteur, A. 37

Leekham, S.R. 38
Liebkham, M.R. 43
Liebowitz Social Anxiety Scale 43
Lord, C. 37

March, J.S. 10
Mataix-Cols, D.M. 117
modelling, tasks/behaviours 24
Mood and Feelings Questionnaire 43
mood, measures of 43
Morris, J. 23
motorbike rating scale 79–83
Mulle, K. 10

NICE 27, 124
non-verbal communication 21–2
normal behaviour 106
normalisation of obsessional thoughts
        58

obsessions 35–6
    defining 61
    vs. worries 58
obsessive compulsive disorder (OCD)
        65
    cognitive components 65–6
    context 63, 64–5
    cycle 59
    definitions 57
    formulation 63–6
    Harold's formulation 67
    OCD definitions worksheet 61
    OCD trap handout 62
    onset 39–40
    parent/carer modelling 45
    psycho-education 49, 57–62
    therapist tips 66
    triggers and maintenance 63, 64–5
    What is OCD? worksheet 60
    see also cognitive behaviour therapy
        (CBT); exposure and response
        prevention (ERP); OCD
        assessment
Obsessive-Compulsive Inventory-
        Revised (OCI-R) 42
OCD assessment
    asking questions 36

OCD assessment *cont.*
  clients unable to describe feelings
    41–2
  client's views/experience 34
  family involvement/accommodation
    43
  general guidance 31–2
  key considerations 32, 43–4
  measures of mood 43
  measures of social anxiety 43
  meeting significant others 34–5
  mental state and functioning 34
  rapport building 33
  repetitive behaviours 37–41
  session routine 33–5
  standardised self-report 42–4
  structured clinical interview 35–6
  symptom assessment 33
  therapist tips 44–5

parent/carer modelling 45
Patient Health Questionnaire-9
  (PHQ-9) 43
practical living skills 14
Prior, M.R. 38
psycho-education 49, 57–62
Purdon, C. 121

questions
  during assessment 36
  open/closed 20–1

rapport building 33
relapse prevention
  action plans 121–2
  family/carer involvement 121
  follow-up sessions 123–4
  golden rules 122
  introducing 117–19
  residual symptoms 122–3
  Tanisha's action plan 126–7
  template for relapse prevention plan
    128–9
  tips 124–5
  trigger identification 119–20
  warning signs 120–1
relaxation 79–83

repetitive behaviours
  distinguishing from OCD 37–41
  tips 26
residual symptoms 122–3
resources 131–2
restricted repetitive behaviours (RRB)
  37–41
Revised Children's Anxiety and
  Depression Scale 43
rewards 111
ritual replacement 64, 111
routines 65
Russell, A.J. 9
Rutter, M. 37

Simpson, H.B. 84
SMART goals 53
social anxiety 64
  measures of 43
social interaction 13
  tips 25
Spence Children's Anxiety Scale 43
Spence, S.H. 43
Spitzer, R.L. 43
standardised self-report 42–4
Steer, R.A. 43
Steketee, G.S. 10, 106
stress, as trigger 119–20
structured clinical interview 35–6
symptom assessment 33
symptom checklists 35, 44

talking therapies, adaptation 20–4
Tanisha 12, 40–1, 103, 107, 110, 113
  exposure hierarchy 102–3
  relapse prevention plan 126–7
terminology
  anxiety 73
  autism spectrum disorder (ASD)
    15–16
theories of ASD 14
Theory of Mind 14, 99
therapeutic situations
  adaptation 20–4
  communication preferences 16
  daily living 17
  interests and routines 16–17

overview 14
    terminology 15–16
therapeutic style, tips 25–6
therapists, organisation 23–4
'thoughts-feelings-behaviour'
    framework 27–9
thoughts, in CBT 27
timeframes, ERP 108–9
tips
    exposure and response prevention
        (ERP) 114–15
    OCD assessment 44–5
    relapse prevention 124–5
    therapeutic style 25–6
Top, N. 106
treatment
    setting 24
    structure and timing 23
trigger identification 119–20
Turner, M. 37

Uher, R. 42–3
Uljarevic, M. 38

vignettes see Harold; Tanisha
visual aids 10–11, 24, 58–9, 84–5

warning signs, relapse prevention
    120–1
Whiteside, S.P. 108
Wilhelm, S. 10
Williams, J.B. 43
worksheets
    body maps 46–7
    individual ASD 18–19
    Tanisha's relapse prevention plan
        126–7
    template for relapse prevention plan
        128–9

Yale-Brown Obsessive Compulsive
    Scale – Symptom Checklist
    (Y-BOCS) 35–6